CRYSTAL PALACE
NORWOOD HEIGHTS
A Pictorial Record

Foresters' Hall, Westow Street

Opened in 1930 this impressive building, in keeping with other local styles, was the social centre for the Ancient Order of Foresters. It had meeting rooms, a dance hall and an adjoining stage with dressing rooms. From the early 1900's Mr Stone's 'Temperance Dining Rooms' had occupied the site. After the 1939-45 War it underwent a number of changes: in 1955 it was the premises of Edwards Pure Sweets, later those of Cowlindex, an office equipment supply firm. In 1970 when the premises became vacant the CPTCA proposed to Croydon Council that it should be used as a Community Arts Centre. Instead the building was leased in 1971 as a Crown Court dealing with the overflow from Croydon Quarter Sessions. At the same time adjacent cottages were demolished to make car-parking facilities for the Court. Now the building is vacant once more: what is its future to be? BD

Audrey Hammond 4·88

CRYSTAL PALACE NORWOOD HEIGHTS
A Pictorial Record

Audrey Hammond and Brian Dann

CRYSTAL PALACE TRIANGLE COMMUNITY ASSOCIATION

First edition published by the Croydon
Society, 1988
Second edition published by the Crystal
Palace Triangle Community Association, 1989
Copyright this publication
© Crystal Palace Triangle Community
Association 1989

British Cataloguing in Publication Data
Hammond, Audrey
Crystal Palace, Norwood Heights: a pictorial
record.
1. Upper Norwood (London, England)
   – History
2. London (England) – History
I. Title II. Dann, Brian
  942.1'91 DA685.U6

ISBN 0 9502866 2 1
Designed by Mike Conrad
Photoset by Input Typesetting Ltd
and Delwest Graphics
Litho origination
by Scantone Graphics Ltd.
Printed by Evedale Ltd. (Tadberry Group)

CONTENTS

SPONSORS

The CRYSTAL PALACE TRIANGLE COMMUNITY ASSOCIATION with the Croydon Society wishes to acknowledge and thank the following for their generous sponsorship and support of this book:

MAJOR FINANCIAL SPONSORS

AD SUMMA NITAMUR

London Borough of Croydon

angloschool, Church Road

OCS Group Limited PLC

Portland Homes Limited

Crystal Palace Triangle
Community Association

Joanna's, Westow Hill

OTHER SPONSORS

Croydon Society

Crystal Palace Foundation

Goodliffe Estates Limited PLC

Greenwich Printmakers

Donald Harris

Elizabeth Morris

National Westminster Bank PLC

Norwood Society

The Picture Palace, Westow Street

Stones of Streatham

Hamptons Levens

Begg Williamson & Co

ACKNOWLEDGEMENTS

Assistance with the general production of the book, and associated support activities.

Miss D Andrews

Len and Sally Blomstrand CPTCA

Gerald Bowthorpe

Stella Boyes CPTCA

Mo Farrer CPTCA

Collins Reprise

Philippa and Andrew Fewster of Pylon

Mrs R Fost

Graveney Art, Norbury

Francis Hammond

Miss C Heynes

The late D H Jackson

Jack Law

The late Geoffrey Manning, Norwood Society

Peter Margerison of Quicksilver

V Mears

Ken Middleton

Mrs J Morrison

'Samuel Pickwick Esq'

Dr J Pryor JP

Mrs Jane Royce

Robert Royce, who originally proposed the book

Mrs Pat Scott, Chief Librarian, Upper Norwood Library

Jerry Savage, Reference Librarian

David Thrower

Thurston of Bromley.

and many others.

Those who lent Audrey's original paintings:
Mr and Mrs M Berger
Mr and Mrs J Brock
Mr W Bunyan
Mrs J Cotton
Mr and Mrs A Hart
Mr and Mrs F Hynds
Mr and Mrs W Kemp
Mr and Mrs J Price
Mr and Mrs A Reid
Mrs V Swales
Mrs E Wood
The Headmistress, Sydenham High School, GPDST.

Scantone Graphics Limited

Evedale Ltd (part of the Tadberry Group) for printing.

Thanks are also due to a number of other individuals and groups in particular Robin Redsull and the Croydon Society who greatly assisted the first edition of this book. Also local authorities, amenity groups and societies, businesses and many other individuals.

The authors particularly wish to thank the Crystal Palace Foundation for permission to reproduce the map shown on page 92 and the Director of Recreation, London Borough of Bromley for permission to reproduce on page 93 the map forming part of the Borough's Draft Development Plan for Crystal Palace Park, published in 1986.

The Crystal Palace Museum on Anerley Hill, created by the Crystal Palace Foundation and opened in 1988.

This book is dedicated
to all those who love the area,
to those in the past who created its character,
to those in the present who are helping to conserve it,
and to our children, to help them remember it.

Woodland Road

The authors would like to add for this edition
a special dedication to the memory of
Geoffrey Manning, secretary of the Norwood Society
who dedicated so much of his time and enthusiasm to the
history of Norwood

LIST OF COLOUR PICTURES

FOREWORD

Mr Speaker

SPEAKER'S HOUSE

WESTMINSTER

SW1A 0AA

Dear Reader,

I willingly declare my interest in what has always been my favourite part of Norwood! Its charming Victorian shops and buildings are memorials to the glory of its past, when, high above the fogs and smogs of London, it was a fashionable and healthy place to live.

Audrey Hammond's pictures capture so much of the essential charm of the area which needs to be conserved by bold and imaginative planning and development.

I warmly commend the book, not only as an attractive record of the past, but as an inspiration for the future.

Bernard Weatherill

◀ **Cherry Tree in former garden of 38 Hamlet Road**

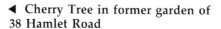

11

INTRODUCTION

This is a partial record; it cannot pretend to be anything else. Partial in that it necessarily reflects the interests and enthusiasms of its authors. Partial too, in that it does not pretend to be anything like a comprehensive record of either history, places or people. Rather, by expressing our declared interests we hope to share them with our readers and so to kindle a matching interest in one or other aspect of the Crystal Palace Triangle and the surrounding area. The essential charm of the place, which is so loved by those of us who know it well, has provided the inspiration for the pictures, the text and the layout.

Making pictures or poems is a very personal business for the artist: it is a means of expressing feelings about things which move her or him especially. For viewers of the pictures or readers of the poems there is the pleasure and satisfaction to be obtained from experiencing works which express feelings about a subject, which help them to find truths about which they previously felt hazy or unsure, or which show them aspects of a familiar subject of which they were unaware.

We hope that you will enjoy and use this book and that it will provide a record of interest to all those who live, work and shop in the area, and to those who until now have merely passed through on their way to other destinations. All the figures in the pictures are portraits of real people; readers are invited to identify them! More than that: we want to encourage all our readers to make their own observations on details to be spotted above familiar shopfronts, to delve more deeply into local history than we have been able to in this short volume, and to contribute their own recollections and in general take a more active interest in their surroundings.

◀ **The Triangle from the Palace**

13

A UNIQUE PART OF LONDON

London's enormous urban spread looks from high-flying aircraft like a single faint blot on the landscape. On the map too, it all appears as grey and anonymous as the grey tone used on this first map. A closer look shows that it is made up of hundreds of small townships, each with its own distinguishable appearance and character.

Crystal Palace, with its compact concentration of shops, cafés, restaurants, pubs, churches and church halls, library, doctors' clinics, and offices is one of these. The large Crystal Palace Park and the associated Sports Centre and Caravan Harbour, and its good rail and bus connections make it obviously unique. But it has a hidden history of its own not always known to its own inhabitants, let alone the numerous visitors, both British and foreign, who are attracted to the area for a variety of reasons. Once a densely wooded ridge at the south-eastern edge of the Thames basin, it was by turns a hunting ground, the haunt of gypsies and highwaymen, a country resort and smugglers' hideaway, a staging-post and a country village surrounded by woodlands and commons. It began to develop as a shopping and supply centre for the rich families who settled in the area during the 18th and early 19th centuries. It developed further prosperity in the 1860s after the Crystal Palace was reopened here in 1854. This gave the area a new name and a character of its own, not only in the styles of many of the new houses, but also in the arched shopfronts reflecting the arches of the Palace itself.

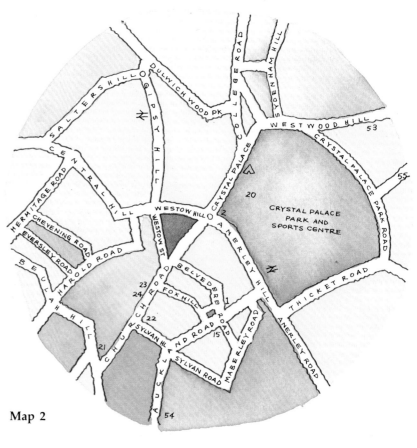

Map 2

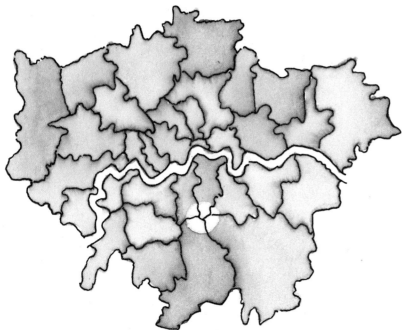

Map 1

THE PLACE

We are talking about the general area in the circle roughly a mile in radius shown on Map 2 which is centred on the ancient site of the 'Vicar's Oak' or, in modern terms, from the centre of the roundabout at the junction of Anerley Hill, Church Road, Crystal Palace Parade and Westow Hill.

Notice how it lies at the extreme corners of no fewer than five London Boroughs. The map only shows these administrative boundaries in modern terms, but maps dating back to 1800 and records going back to the 13th century and earlier show much the same state of affairs. This accounts for many, but by no means all, of the difficulties in finding solutions to the various problems which have arisen as the area has changed over the centuries. A comparatively recent phase as a rather tired suburb suffering from planning blight has led to its present state when it could well be poised for a renascence, with its proliferation of restaurants echoing the earlier days of tea-rooms.

TOPOGRAPHY

But to explain why or how the place gets its character, we must look at the lie of the land, and its history. The whole area is under-laid by London clay, some 400 to 480 feet thick, which formed as mud at the bottom of a sea that covered south-eastern England some 50 million years ago in the Eocene epoch. Scattered through the clay are small beds of gravel and flint nodules, and many fossil remains, including those of sharks, shellfish and subtropical palms. During later ages south-eastern England was lifted up and folded to form the Thames basin. Later the rigours of the Ice Age drastically changed both the land-scape and its flora and fauna. As a result of such geological activi-ties, a two-mile long, 300-feet high ridge was formed which now stretches from the BBC television mast at its north-eastern end to the IBA mast at its southwestern point. The whole area slopes more or less steeply away from this ridge.

Upper Norwood's only named stream, the Effra, is to be seen no more. It used to rise as a spring somewhere in the area of the recreation ground bordered by Eversley Road and Chevening

Road and flow via Dulwich and Brixton to join the Thames at Vauxhall. During the excavation of the site of the Central Hill estate, an underground river was found which may have been the waters of the Effra; the local historian Alan Warwick recorded hearing the rushing of underground waters at the lowest point of Hermitage Road.

THE PICTURES

The locations of the pictures can be found by reference to this larger scale map which shows the street network around the Triangle at the heart of the circle on the previous map. Where items of interest lie somewhat outside this area their general location is indicated.

Map 3

Map 4

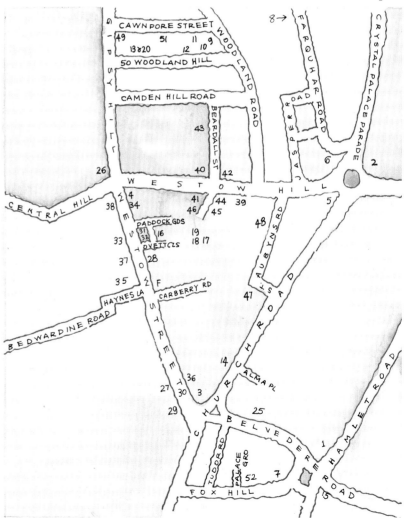

TOBY ALE

WHITE HART

CHARRINGTON

◄ The 'White Hart'

At the Church Road/Westow Street junction stands the 'White Hart' marking the entrance to the Triangle. The present Tyrolean-style brick building dates from 1868 and was designed by Sextus Dyball, an architect who had arranged the enlargement of the previous building in 1861. Several large houses in similar style in the area are also his.

Notice the unique cast-iron arched shopfront of Helen Terry's Ladies' Hairdressers which is now, alas, no more, having been replaced by an anonymous office frontage. And the Gents' loo: closed in 1971, and preserved as a sort of municipal flower display, once happily taken over by Cow Parsley!

(An earlier long two-storey building of weather-boarded construction occupied the 'White Hart' site from the early 1800s. This had bow windows surrounded by chains supported on posts. The inn sign stood several yards in front on a stout timber mast next to a pump from which water was sold at one (old) penny a bucket, or twopence for a large wheeled tub which was provided for customers. Hay was also available for horses. The original building left traces which stood for many years without much alteration. In Church Road there was a small weather-boarded structure which once formed part of the original even though it was no longer part of the same premises. Sadly this was demolished as recently as 1985. On the other side of the road from the old pub was a striking entrance flanked on either side by the enormous jawbones of a whale. One passed through this to the Tea-Gardens which also formed part of the pub's facilities. There were cosy arbours around the gardens, a bowling green in the centre and stables at the back. On the Westow Street side there is another trace: a large pitched roofed 'garage' with weather-boarded flanks, with tall doors surely capable of accommodating a stagecoach if required. This 'Coach House' too, judging by maps and photographs, formed part of the original 'White Hart'.) BD

▲ The 'Holly Bush'

The pub has won awards for having the best kept cellars, and was one of the earliest subjects for Audrey Hammond's pictures. BD

▲ The 'Cambridge'

This fine and unusual pub, built in the 1860s on the acutely angled corner between Church Road and Westow Hill, forms part of a terrace with distinctively rounded window-mouldings on its upper storeys (see the line drawing on page 27).

The fine ceramic-tiled exterior of the pub was 'listed' by the GLC.

Also in this picture you can see the facade above the shops on the opposite side of Church Road. This is the sole remnant of the imposing 'Royal Crystal Palace Hotel' which for many years occupied the entire corner of Church Road and Anerley Hill. In later years the Church Road frontage was sold off and shop premises created at street level. The remaining 'Crystal Palace Hotel' was badly damaged during the 1939–45 war and was replaced by 'The Sportsman'. BD

▶ The 'White Swan', cabmen's kiosk and Crystal Palace Parade

This prospect is what is left of the splendid approach to the Palace gates which can just be seen on the right. The 'White Swan', minus its top floor, was a casualty of wartime bombs. The pub is the second on this site; the original was a coaching inn with large tea-gardens before the Palace was erected here. Earlier still there was a smithy here.

The Vicar's Oak marking the meeting point of several parishes stood at the spot where the traffic roundabout is now.

The distinctive little kiosk, once an office for the local horse-cabs and later a tramway office has been demolished only recently. So much for suggestions for incorporating it into an improved entrance to the Park at this point! BD

WESTOW HILL
SE19

TELEPHONE

19

▲ 'Charcoal Burner's Cottage'
Set in what appeared to be a leafy glade rather than an ordinary garden, it seemed far too grand a place to have been the home of folk who more likely lived in hovels or even 'benders', this house was neverless widely known locally as 'The Charcoal Burner's Cottage'. Alas, despite pleas for its preservation it was dismissed as a building of no particular architectural significance and demolished in 1971, so removing another building contributing to the overall character of the area. BD

HISTORY: a brief chronology

'Unwritten history' is a contradiction in terms – but it forms an important part of the story of both the early years of Norwood and its middle life, well into the 19th century. Few archaeological traces provide any concrete evidence. Roman bronze and copper artefacts on Sydenham Hill, coin hoards at Whitehorse Manor (9th-century Anglo-Saxon and Arabic coins) and at Beulah Hill (14th-century silver coins) give hints: the need to protect ill- or well-gotten gains from predacious eyes, trade routes to Europe and beyond, dark deeds in the wild woods . . .

The local topography would have made the area an ideal site for one or more hill-forts in prehistoric times and there was a hill-fort at Dawson's Heights in Lordship Lane and a tumulus on the site of the nearby Telephone Exchange. No evidence of either has yet been unearthed in the Triangle area, though some prehistoric artefacts have been found in the gravel beds along Church Road.

The Great North Wood, which gave Norwood its name, contrasted with the Great South Wood of the Weald which formed the centre of England's iron industry before the Industrial Revolution. Clay is ideally suited to the growth of deep-rooted trees, such as the English oak, but being a cold wet soil, it was not ideally suited for permanent settlements. Consequently for many centuries the whole district was covered in dense woodlands (with interspersed commons of rough pasture), providing fuel, timber and rough grazing.

From London's earliest years the practice of burning coal has periodically led to bans or restrictions on its use, as the air became increasingly polluted with smoke. (The earliest of these appears to be an edict of 1273, and the latest the Clean Air Act of 1956). The result was to create a continually increasing demand for charcoal for cooking and heating, and the woodlands around the capital began to be coppiced for this reason. (Coppicing was the practice of cutting the underwood of thickets specially grown for the purpose). Charcoal burning was a local rural industry, and bundles of charcoal were regularly delivered to London's markets. Charcoal burners were known as colliers: Grimme the Collier of Croydon is much mentioned as a stereotype in plays and skits from the 16th century onwards.

Timber was the chief constructional material for ships, for carts and carriages, and for buildings in pre-industrial Surrey and Kent. The stout hearts of oaks of the great North Wood formed the stout timbers of the British Navy over the centuries. Sir Francis Drake's 'Golden Hind' was built of Norwood trees. Most local early building was of weather-boarded construction (timber-framed buildings with an outside covering of overlapping boards nailed horizontally), because this made the fullest use of locally available materials. Despite the presence of the underlying clay, extensive brickfields only made their appearance in the 19th century when the woodland had been largely cleared.

The Lords of the Manor (of whom the chief was the Archbishop of Canterbury) had the rights of hunting and of felling useful timber trees. The custom of the manor was to lay open the coppices of Norwood for the benefit of the tenants every seven years when they could exercise their right of 'estovers', namely 'to fell and carry away all bushes, furze, ash, hazel, willow and hornbeam but not timber (ie oak)'. The roots of fallen and felled trees belonged by custom to the poor.

The plentiful acorns and roots provided grazing for all sorts of animals both wild and domesticated. These provided both sport (hunting for Royalty and the Lord of the Manor) and sustenance for the yeomen and gypsies of the Great North Wood. The district was famous for its gypsies, a fact remembered in the names of many local roads. Many local family names in historical records are those of gypsies. The woods may have offered refuge to the panic-stricken citizens of Southwark and Lambeth, who fled from the Great Plague of 1665–6, and several open spaces in the area have the probably unjustified reputation of being mass graves of plague victims. The woods certainly formed cover and comfort for outlaws and until well into the 19th century, the area was justifiably notorious, as a haunt of smugglers. But such folk left no recorded history. There is only the possibility of recovering some oral history, as the Crystal Palace Foundation is doing for the Palace.

The earliest written records referring to this area date from the reign of the Wessex Anglo-Saxon King Eadwig (955–959), granting lands in Battersea to a certain Lyfing, with the right to graze pigs in the Penge woods – accounting for the fact that for nearly 1,000 years Penge formed part of the parish of Battersea, a district without benefit of woodlands. Ensuing records are summarised in the following brief chronology:

1066	Battersea and, with it, Penge, granted to the Abbot of Westminster by William the Conqueror.
1085	Domesday Book refers to: 'That part of the Great North Wood within the parish of Croindene, and a peculiar to Canterbury, given for the Archbishop's pleasure, for his hunting, for fuel and pannage (pasturage) for 200 swine.'
1100	Henry I had a hunting lodge on the site of 'Kingswood House'.
1272	Roger de Northwood held lands in the vicinity.
1368	Lands in what is now South Norwood granted to Edward III's shield-bearer ('White Horse Wood').
1540	The Elder Oak (marker tree formerly on the Lambeth boundary at the corner of Elder Road) said to have been cut down. Later records suggest that the tree or its successor survived until much later.
1550	Boundary disputes between the Manors of Croydon and Penge, during the annual beating of bounds at Rogationtide. This practice dating from the time of Avitus, Bishop of Vienna in 800, was the method used to familiarise people with the parish boundaries. The choir and congregation would process around the parish bounds, the corners of which were marked by named trees, such as the Elder Oak and the Vicar's Oak (which marked the boundary point of four parishes).
1566	*Grimme the Collier of Croydon*: a comedy by Richard Edwards.
1594– 1733	Windmill at the top of Knight's Hill, Crown Point, served local farms.
1645	First written reference to mineral springs (at Streatham?).
1646	Cromwellian survey refers to 'Norwood Heights cut about, in 830 acres only 80 timber trees and 9200 oaken pollards remain'.

1652	John Evelyn, the diarist, dragged from his horse and mugged 'near the Vicars Oak'. His assailants were captured and his property restored.
1668	Samuel Pepys mentions in his diary a visit his wife and friends paid to the Norwood gypsies. The traditional meeting place between Londoners and the gypsies was the 'Horns Tavern' adjacent to the present 'Horns' public house on Knight's Hill.
1675	John Evelyn visited the area; including Sydenham Wells near the site of St Philip's Church, by Sydenham Wells Park.
1678	An apothecary, seeking mistletoe for his potions was said to have felled a boundary oak and to have broken both his legs as a consequence.
1689	The Vicar's Oak referred to by the author and antiquary John Aubrey.
1690	'The Sycamores', Beulah Hill first built.

The Sycamores Beulah Hill

1700	'Northwood Common' said to be less than 200 acres in extent.
1740	Margaret Finch, Queen of the Gypsies, died aged 104.
1746	Rocque's Survey published, showing the Great North Wood, Bewleys Farm, Croxted Lane, Sydenham Wells, etc.
1756	Inclosure Act to ensure adequate supplies of timber for ship construction for the Navy.
1762	Original 'Rose and Crown' built at the top of Knight's Hill.
1768	Old Bridget Finch, Queen of the Gypsies and niece of Margaret, died. Buried in Dulwich.
1772	Lord Thurlow acquired Knight's Hill Farm for his mistress, Polly Humphreys, and thus started the acquisition of the extensive Thurlow estate.
1773	Inclosure Act 'to secure adequate food supplies'.
1775	Augustus Hervey, Earl of Bristol, set up home with Mary Nesbitt at a 'cottage' on the wooded slopes of Central Hill. She was the widow of a member of the prominent de Crespigny family of Camberwell. He had previously made an unfortunate marriage. The couple had many influential friends, including

George Rose, Secretary to the Treasury, and William Pitt. Indeed the Privy Council, including George IIII, met at the house, which had been developed into a substantial mansion, 'Norwood House'. The gravel pit was turned into an ornamental lake and large stables were added.

1777	*The Norwood Gypsies*: pantomime at Covent Garden.
1778	'The Gypsy House', an inn near the habitual camping place of the Gypsy Queen, using her portrait as its inn sign, was first mentioned in records, although Margaret Finch had evidently lived there until her death in 1740. Violent storms reported in the Norwood area with hailstones 8–9 inches in diameter!
1780	The Surrey Militia, recruited locally, involved in quelling the Gordon Riots. Houses on Beulah Hill erected, one on the foundations of a 17th-century dwelling.
1781	Norwood first described as 'a village scattered round an extensive wild common' in J. Bew's *The Ambulator*.
1790	Charcoal burning ceased to be recorded as a local industry.
1797	Waste lands of Norwood enclosed and leased to Dr Moore and others.
1800	'The Woodman' first opened on Westow Hill, probably as a simple ale-house.
1801	Croydon Inclosure Act: Ecclesiastical Commissioners confirmed as great landowners in the district.

In the late 18th century better roads meant more reliable transport and, well into the 19th century, 'Norwood Heights' was a place of refreshment and recreation, particularly to travel-weary passengers and horses alike, having toiled up the slopes to and from Surrey and Kent. Watermen too made it a place of resort after the rigours of their work and particularly, it was said, after the annual Doggett's Coat and Badge race, and as a place to retire at the end of their working lives. Several public houses date from these times, and tea-gardens abounded.

About the turn of the century a number of significant events occurred – not all of them local – but all symptomatic of the changing times, and all having a profound effect on the district and its inhabitants. The population of London doubled during the 18th century. It had almost quadrupled again by the end of the 19th. The result was more air pollution, overcrowding and insanitary conditions. Those who could afford it moved farther and farther out towards the southern outskirts of London for the clean air and inspiring views. These households, their servants, carriages and horses required the services of local corn merchants, chandlers, blacksmiths, farriers and the like.

At the same time, all around London as elsewhere in the country, common lands were being enclosed to form more productive and profitable farms. As a consequence numbers of people who had managed to make a living on the land with subsistence farming were uprooted and rendered incapable of supporting themselves. Local parish charities could not cope, and so the Workhouse was devised to give wholesome employment under stringent conditions, thereby ensuring that the poor were 'deserving' of society's charity.

The old horse ferries over the Thames, and the cramped Old London Bridge, were replaced by new bridges bearing metalled roads suitable for faster and more capacious horse transport. Locally, the death of Lord Thurlow led to the break-up of his estate and the possibility of new urban development in the area.

1804	Francis Campbell, later to become founder of the Royal Normal College for the Blind, moved to Sydenham.
1806	The eminent lawyer and politician Lord Thurlow died. Lambeth Manor Inclosure Act.
1808	Norwood Common Inclosure Act. Gypsy House demolished.
1809	Croydon Canal opened. This ran from West Croydon, through South Norwood, Anerley, Forest Hill and soon to the Grand Surrey Canal. (The sole remaining portion of this canal forms the main feature of Betts Park on Anerley Hill and its reservoir formed what is now South Norwood Lake). An interesting booklet by Ken Maggs and Paul De'athe: *South Norwood and the Croydon Canal* gives further details. The Thurlow estate (which had proved difficult to dispose of) was broken up by an Act of Parliament which enabled roads to be driven through it.
1810	Enclosure roads (Elder Road, Gipsy Road, Gipsy Hill and Salters Hill) driven through Norwood Common to open up the area for development. House of Industry for the Infant Poor (Workhouse) set up in Elder Road. Eventually extended to become 'Elderwood' and 'Norwood House'. Allocation of portions of Norwood Common to existing landowners in proportion to their existing holdings.
1813	Windmill erected on site behind 30 Westow Hill. This mill had an inordinate number of tenants during its 40 years of existence. The last one, a Mr Pocknell, eventually gave up business as a miller in 1853 and settled down as a grocer and corn chandler.
1815	Gypsies of Norwood apprehended as vagrants and sent in three coaches to prison.
1818	830 acres of 'waste land' enclosed at Norwood. 1,000 inhabitants, 160 houses. Francis Meagre recorded as the owner of 'White Horse, Beucham (sic), Norwood Hill and Blind Corner'.
1820	Chapel in Chapel Road, Lower Norwood, opened, built on land donated by Mr Salter. At about the same time the Lower Norwood Nonconformist Day School was opened. A Dr Leese held pastures in Upper and Lower Norwood. The 'Rose and Crown' reopened in more substantial premises at Crown Point.
1822	Parish church of St Luke's, Lower Norwood, built at a cost of £13,000. The architect was Francis Bedford.
1824	Cornerstone incorporated into building in Woodman's Yard.
1825	Last record of the existence of the Vicar's Oak. St Luke's Church consecrated and parish school opened in Elder Road.
1827	All Saints' Church foundation stone laid by Lady Carey, wife of Viscount Falkland. The church was first designated as a Chapel of Ease to take the larger number of parishioners now living in the Norwood area.
1829	All Saints' Church consecrated. Edmund Harden MA installed as Curate.
1830	St Bartholomew's Church, Westwood Hill, built. Joseph Paxton designed the gardens for 'The Wood', a villa at 16 Sydenham

Hill, the property of his patron and friend, the Duke of Devonshire, nearly 20 years before he conceived the original idea for the Crystal Palace for the 1851 Exhibition in Hyde Park.

1831	Beulah Spa (designed and landscaped by Decimus Burton) opened to the public by John Davidson Smith.
1835	'The Park Hotel' opened in premises which had been the home of the notorious Mary Nesbitt (see the section on People in this book). All Saints' School opened.
1836	Croydon Canal opened.
1837	West Norwood Cemetery opened.
1839	London & Croydon Railway opened.
1840	'The Tyrol', a large chalet-style house built in Church Road next to where the 'Queen's Hotel would be built.
1841	Anerley Tea Gardens opened.
1844	Croydon Atmospheric Railway opened.
1845	All Saints' Church enlarged and made a Parish Church. First vicar: Rev. Edmund Harden MA.
1848	Roman Catholic Orphanage of Our Lady, Central Hill, opened in premises of former 'Park Hotel'.

Detail over doorway, Virgo Fidelis Convent

1849 St Aubyn's School became the Central London District Industrial School, training boys to become mariners. A Mr Leach disappeared in the local woods and was never seen again!

1850 'Harefield', a large house on Anerley Hill built; now a 'listed' building.

The Great Exhibition of 1851 in Hyde Park provided the original reason for the development of the Crystal Palace by Paxton and Fox Henderson and Partners. The proceeds of that exhibition, some £186,000, were sufficient to provide for the purchase of land for the complex of Museums and Imperial College at South Kensington under the patronage of Prince Albert, Prince Consort to Queen Victoria. Paxton and his fellow directors of the Crystal Palace were inspired by similar lofty objectives in seeking to re-erect the Crystal Palace in enlarged form to produce a unique cultural centre to provide both entertainment and instruction to the public. They chose a site in Sydenham, the property of Leo Schuster, who happened to be a director of the London, Brighton and South Coast Railway Company. (Samuel Laing, the chairman of both companies, inaugurated the construction by supervising the erection of the first pillar of the Palace on the Sydenham site.)

Not only was Europe scoured for what was then considered to be the best of sculpture, but several colleges were endowed to give instruction in the arts and sciences. Hence, among others, there was a School of Art, a School of Music and Singing, and a School of Engineering. Only the latter appears to have survived into the 20th century; it was housed by the base of the South Tower. The other schools had some notable instructors, including the youthful Arthur (later Sir Arthur) Sullivan.

Unfortunately for these noble aims, they took no account of Sunday Observance, one of the facts of Victorian life. For many years the Crystal Palace was closed on the one day when ordinary working people would have been free to attend. So the very public the directors had hoped to reach was excluded from both its various courts and galleries and the Schools of Art and Science.

1852 'Rockhills', home of Joseph Paxton and of successive Managers of the Crystal Palace, built at the top of Westwood Hill. The first column of the new Crystal Palace and Central Hill Baptist Church erected. Norwood New Town built to accommodate the hundreds of labourers and glaziers who would build the new Palace. The creation of this 'ghetto' was to provide many problems of law and order in the years to come!

1853 Knight's Hill Wesleyan Methodist church opened.

1854 Crystal Palace opened more than a year later than had been planned. Crystal Palace (Low Level) Station of the London Brighton and South Coast Railway opened by Queen Victoria. Police Station open on Gipsy Hill (the building has been converted to flats). The Central London District Industrial School (training poor children for the merchant navy among other careers and featuring a complete set of masts and rigging) moved from its site to make way for St Aubyns Church and the development extending from St Aubyns Road to the 'Cambridge' public house.

1855 Large water tanks erected to the North of the Palace to supply water to the upper foundations and jets of the Palace grounds. William Beale, with the support of Scott Russell, arranged the first orchestral concert at the Palace under the auspices of the New Philharmonic Society.

1856 Opening of West End & Crystal Palace Railway. (Lower Norwood and Gipsy Hill stations). Grand opening of the completed waterworks and fountains which Paxton hoped would outshine those of Versailles.

1857 Construction of the 'Queen's Hotel' in Church Road completed in grounds which originally stretched down to where Eversley Road now runs. This famous hotel has had many notable guests over the years: Florence Nightingale, the Duke of Wellington, John Bright MP, Emile Zola, Kaiser Wilhelm, King Faisal among them. The German Crown Prince Frederick stayed here for his health in 1887, his doctors assuring him ''Norwood air is the finest anywhere in the world''. Playing fields were laid out in the Crystal Palace grounds. The first of many Handel Festivals was held at the Palace.

1858 Gypsy encampment on Gipsy Hill. New shops built on Church Road. Saturday concerts started at the Palace. The Crystal Palace Art Union formed.

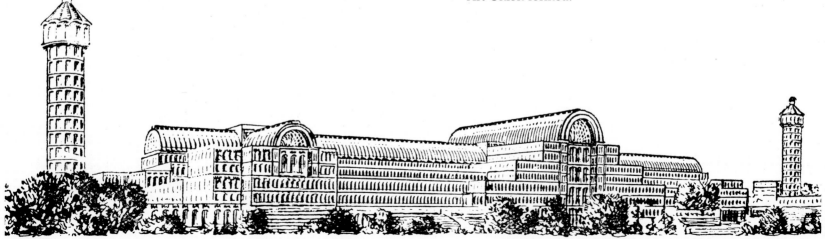

1859 'The Lawns', Beulah Hill, replaced the now defunct Spa.

1860 First Brass Band contest at Crystal Palace. All Saints' Church completed with a spire. Further additions to complete the 'Queen's Hotel'.

1861 The 'White Hart' hotel enlarged. North Transept of Crystal Palace damaged by fire.

1862 Arthur Sullivan's incidental music to *The Tempest* had its first performance at Crystal Palace. 'Iron church' set up on Gipsy Hill a little way up the hill from the present site to serve 'the new District of Christ Church, part of the Parish of St Luke's, Lower Norwood.'

1863 First National Fire Engine competition at Crystal Palace.

1864 Atmospheric Railway experiments at Crystal Palace by Mr Ramell. C. T. Brock & Company's firework factory established at South Norwood. All Saints' School enlarged. Garibaldi, the Italian patriot, stayed in the area, living with friends on Beulah Hill and visiting the Crystal Palace.

1865 Vice-Admiral Fitzroy, founder of the Meteorolical Office and former commander of HMS 'Beagle' (famous for its voyage with Charles Darwin as Naturalist), dies at his home in Church Road. Crystal Palace (Upper Level) station (and the 'Italian' subway linking it with the Palace) opened as a terminus of the London Chatham and Dover Railway. The first of many 'Brock's Benefit' firework displays.

1866 St Philip's Church, Wells Road, Sydenham built on the former site of Sydenham Wells Spa. Dulwich College built (designed by Charles Barry) Serious fire destroys the North Wing of Crystal Palace, never restored. Gypsies still reported as camping out in the local brickworks. Foundation stone of the new stone building of Christ Church, Gipsy Hill laid.

1867 Christ Church consecrated by a Canon of Winchester, in whose diocese the church then was. The first local bank, a branch of Barclay's, opened in Westow Hill. First archery competition at the Palace. Crystal Palace bowmen formed. Annual archery competitions continued to be held here for many years.

1868 Compulsory Church Rates abolished by Act of Parliament. Fire Station opened at Crystal Palace. First performance of Schubert's Unfinished Symphony and some hitherto 'lost' parts of 'Rosamunde' at the Palace. Loop line connecting Crystal Palace with Victoria.

1870 Crystal Palace Gas Works opened.

1871 Land forming part of the Crystal Palace grounds sold for housing development and to help to balance the books of the Company. The United Land Company started laying out roads around Gipsy Hill. 'Little Menlo', Beulah Hill, built: residence of Col. Gourard, colleague of Thomas Alva Edison and his European representative. Named after the New Jersey head-quarters of Edison's organisation, it was the first house in Great Britain to have a telephone. The house was said to have formed the model for 'Pondicherry Lodge' in Conan Doyle's classic detective story 'The Sign of Four'.

1872 Crystal Palace School of Practical Engineering opened by J W Wilson. A maze was opened in the Crystal Palace grounds.

1874 Upper Norwood Methodist Church opened in Westow Hill by Joseph Tritton, father of Sir Henry Tritton. First services for the Presbyterian congregation held in the Assembly Rooms adjoining the 'White Hart' hotel. Committee of Enquiry into the affairs of the Crystal Palace Company set up. Woodland Hill Hall built to accommodate the Sunday School, a soup-kitchen and other activities of the Christ Church congregation.

1875 The first building of St John the Evangelist Church assembled at Auckland Road from cast and corrugated iron parts brought from its previous location in Grange Woods. The briefly glorious Upper Norwood Athenaeum society started meetings in the Wesleyan Hall (See the note on Sir Rider Haggard in the People section for an interesting sidelight on this).

1876 'The Woodman' public house rebuilt as a three-storey brick building, to replace the former porticoed hotel with its extensive facilities for stagecoaches. Woodman Yard retained as stables and depot for the many local hansom cabs.

1877 Royal Normal College and Academy of Music for the Blind opened at Westow Street. Baptist Chapel, Chatsworth Way, opened. Charter of the Crystal Palace Company annulled and the company reorganised.

1878 New wing and cloisters for Convent of Our Lady, Central Hill. Foundation stone for the present Church of St John the Evangelist laid. St Andrew's Presbyterian Church, Westow Street, opened. Villas built in Westow Hill. Mission Church of St Jude's and hall built in Berridge Road.

1879 Norwood created as a separate Postal District.

1881 Kingswood Primary School opened. The unusual 'New Jerusalem' Swedenborgian Church, Waldegrave Road, constructed. First (and unsuccessful) Electric Exhibition held at Crystal Palace. Heavy snowfall recorded in the area on July 11.

1881–82 Gipsy Road Baptist Church built and dedicated. Development of Auckland Road. Norwood Cottage Hospital, Hermitage Road, opened 'to deal with the large number of accidents arising at the Crystal Palace'.

'Jack o' the Green' head over doorway in Gipsy Hill

Woodland Road

1883 'Grecian Villa', Beulah Hill (later to become part of St Joseph's College) erected as the palatial home of King Edward VII's bookmaker, Samuel 'Dick (your honest friend)' Fry.

1884 International Exhibition at Crystal Palace. Houses built near the Lower Level station on land sold off by the Crystal Palace Company.

1885 New stable block built for the 'Queen's Hotel'. The 'White Swan' rebuilt. Lower Norwood renamed 'West Norwood'.

1886 Admiral Carey, Viscount Falkland, died. 'The Lad's Rest' opened at 106 Beulah Hill with the objects of 'educating and training destitute Orphan Boys between 8 and 15 years of age'.

1887 Woodland Road (later Paxton) School opened. Consecration of St John the Evangelist Church.

1889 Tower of Christ Church completed. Said at the time to be 'The best church tower in South East London'.

1891 Lantern lecture at the Crystal Palace: 'England Bisected by a Steam Launch', given by Mr N. W. Noakes, official lanternist at the Albert Hall, and a pioneer of scenic photography. The somewhat surrealist title of the lecture referred to a recently completed tour via rivers and canals by Noakes who compiled a complete travelogue of photographic plates.

1892 Great Electrical Exhibition held at Crystal Palace. Electric lighting installed in the Royal Crystal Palace Hotel which stood at the corner of Church Road and Anerley Hill, having facades on both streets. The 'Railway Bell', Cawnpore Street, rebuilt.

1893 Norwood Hospital enlarged by the addition of a new wing. Percy Fitzgerald's book *Victoria's England* recorded: 'The various ascents from Dulwich towards the Palace have a special attraction. The roads are all "green lanes", and in spite of the innumerable villas, never seem to lose their sylvan character. The foliage, the laurels and shrubberies are luxuriant, and the grass abounds; and with it there is a sense of dreamy solitude and an air of contented happiness and tranquillity.' At the age of 71, the acrobat Blondin performs on a tight-rope 60 ft in the air across the South Transept without the benefit of a safety net!

1894 Football pitch, sports ground and racing track created in the Crystal Palace grounds in the filled in North and South basins of Paxton's no longer functioning fountains.

1895 First Football Cup Final played at the Palace. Cup Finals continued to be played at the site until 1914.

1898 London County Cricket Club (Player-manager Dr W G Grace) inaugurated at the Crystal Palace playing fields. Dr Grace lived at 'Parklands' where the Adventure Playground is now.
New organ installed in Christ Church.

1899 Date of carved plaque on the top gable of Upper Norwood Library, Westow Hill.

1900 Upper Norwood Library, Westow Hill officially opened. National Brass Band Championships at the Crystal Palace.

1902 First ascent by an Englishman in a powered balloon made at Crystal Palace.

1903 First Automobile Show at the Crystal Palace.

1906 South Metropolitan Electric Tramcar and Lighting Company started Route No. 5 between West Croydon and Crystal Palace. The trams had to have extra brakes to negotiate Anerley Hill.

1909 Crystal Palace Company bankrupt.

1911 Opening of Norwood Park, Elder Road. First electric trains to Crystal Palace via Sydenham for the great Festival of Empire opened by the new King George V. The Palace and its ground were put up for sale.

1913 The Palace was acquired for the nation and Trustees appointed. The Monograph Film Company took up premises in the Palace outbuildings.

1914–18 For the duration of the first World War the Palace became a Naval training establishment, 'HMS Victory VI'. The Football Club (and the Cup Final with it) moved, never to return.

A window of the original Royal Crystal Palace Hotel, above the Crystal Palace Camping shop.

1919	The Palace became a Demobilisation Station.
1920	Palace reopened by George V who inaugurated the Imperial War Museum which had its home here until 1924 when it moved to its present home in Lambeth.
1923	Fire in the South Wing of the Palace.
1925	Woolworths, the first of the multi-nationals came to Westow Hill in a typical 'Woolworth's' style building.
1926	Norwood Grove opened to the public by the Prince of Wales.
1929	The 'Albany' cinema opened in Church Road. 'Sun Lodge' at the corner of Upper Beulah Hill became the headquarters of the Sun Bathing Society.
1930	The Foresters Hall, Westow Street, opened.
1933	The newly-formed London Passenger Transport Board took over the tram and bus routes.
1936	Opening of Upper Norwood Junior Library and Reading Room by the author A. E. W. Mason. Destruction of the Crystal Palace by fire. Trollybuses replaced the trams on February 9th.
1937	'Albany' cinema reconstructed. Motor racing circuit inaugurated in the Palace grounds.
1938	Branch of Burtons opened by Raymond Montague Burton, the founder's son, in premises in Westow Hill now occupied by Bradleys.
1939	'Albany' cinema became a government food store.
1940	'Royal Crystal Palace Hotel' bombed.
1941–42	The Crystal Palace towers removed, by demolition (South Tower) and by dynamiting (North Tower).
1944	Many local buildings damaged or destroyed by V1 flying bombs and V2 rockets.
1946	Branch line to Crystal Palace Upper Level station closed.
1951	In 'Festival of Britain' year a temporary caravan park was opened. This has grown to the 'Caravan Harbour' run by the Caravan Club of Great Britain since 1969 and accomodating up to 30,000 people in a season. Its position here with good transport connections enables many people who could not otherwise afford it to visit London's many attractions.
1953	Children's Zoo opened at Crystal Palace Park. Coin hoard found at 'Woodlands' estate, Beulah Hill, now at the British Museum.
1954	Crystal Palace High Level Station closed. Erection of the mast of the BBC transmitter started on the site of the 1871 Aquarium.
1956	'Crystal Palace Hotel' opened after rebuilding on part of the site of the former 'Royal Crystal Palace Hotel'. 'Kingswood House', previously the home of Lord Vestey, opened to the public as a Library and Community Centre.
1957	Woodland Hill halls demolished; new Christ Church Parish Hall opened as "Goodliffe Hall' in Highland Road.
1959	Trolleybuses replaced by buses.
1960	Formation of what was to become the Norwood Society. Croydon Council agreed to open Beaulieu heights after pressure from the

Society. The 'Century' cinema, formerly the 'Albany' sold to become a car showroom. 'Rockhills', badly damaged during the War and later by vandalism, demolished. Only the distinctive gateposts remain.

1961	Crystal Palace Upper Level station demolished.
1962	Norwood Society's first exhibition 'Living with the Palace'. Planning permission for a nine-storey block of flats at the top of Anerley Hill refused.
1963	Planning permission refused for multi-storey flats at Crown Point, Beulah Hill and Sylvan Road.
1964	Methodist Church, Westow Hill replaced by a new church in a complex incorporating a Tesco supermarket. National Sports Centre opened by the Duke of Edinburgh.
1965	'The angloschool' language school moved to its present Church Road premises. Every year over a thousand students pass through its doors. The Crystal Palace Ski Slope opened.
1966	Second Norwood Society exhibition. Plans for a new National Exhibition Centre on the old Palace site dropped by GLC.
1967	New All Saints' Schools opened. 'Oxford Arms' pub, Central Hill, demolished. Tour of Upper Norwood for Croydon Chief Officers arranged by Norwood Society.
1968	'Granada' cinema (formerly the 'Rialto'), Church Road, turned into Bingo club. Feasibility study by GLC on Crystal Palace Park development.

The urns above the first floor windows of this shop in Westow Hill denote a hardware shop.

1970	Formation of Crystal Palace Triangle Community Association (CPTCA). Norwood Society organised exhibition 'The Triangle: Dead or Alive?' The Foresters Hall in Westow Street, which could have been an ideal Community Centre, leased by Croydon Council as a Crown Court. Some houses in Church Road renumbered (All Saints' Vicarage, previously numbered 207, became 217).
1971	'Charcoal Burner's Cottage', Fox Hill, demolished in spite of local protests. *Norwood News* offices moved from Church Road. Threat of Ringway 2 removed. Former Headmaster's house (1820) at All Saints' School demolished despite protests.

1972 United Reformed Church formed by merging the congregations of the Congregationalist and Presbyterian Churches. End of motor racing at Crystal Palace circuit. New Post Office Sorting Office off Westow Street. London Borough of Bromley propose demolition of 200 houses around Palace Square. Old All Saints' School buildings demolished in spite of protests. The first edition of *The Phoenix Suburb* by Alan Warwick published. London Borough of Bromley set up Conservation Area between Fox Hill and Anerley Hill.

1973 Upper Norwood Association for Community Care (UNACC) founded by Harry Cardwell. New wing added to the 'Queen's Hotel' on the site of 'The Tyrol'. Harold Road designated as a conservation area.

1974 Crystal Palace 120th Anniversary Festival produced by all local organisations working together. Norwood Society's fourth exhibition. 'The Hole in the Heart'. *Crystal Palace and Norwood Advertiser* and *South London Advertiser* ceased publication. Fire at 'Queen's Hotel'. Boots the Chemists ceased trading at Crystal Palace, after having removed the shop's historic interior to their museum at Nottingham.

1975 Lambeth's Central Hill Estate wins a Housing Award. Sylvan High School opened. Experimental pedestrian precinct in Westow Hill abandoned after three months' trial. Planning permission refused for a block of flats to be erected on the front garden of the Regency house 'Innisfail', Beulah Hill. Cambridges (fishmongers) closed after 30 years trading in Westow Street. The CPTCA started its annual Christmas Day dinner for OAPs.

1976 Harold Road/Church Road area designated a Conservation Area by Croydon. 'Tivoli Lodge' saved from demolition, sold and rehabilitated.

1977 Queen Mary's Boys Club, Westow Street, closed. Dr Barnardo Hostel for Teenagers and Day-Centre for Pre-School Children opened in 'Windermere House'. The Greek Orthodox Church of SS Constantine and Helen consecrated in the building previously housing the Presbyterian congregation. The CPTCA persuaded the London Borough of Croydon to sell a row of Victorian cottages in Carberry Road on restoration leases rather than demolish them. Alas, the lack of any preservation order on their fronts allowed their character to be lost.

1978 Redevelopment proposed for Westow Street, the Paddock and St Aubyn's Road. Proposals to build Water Pumping Station at Beaulieu Heights dropped after protests by the Norwood Society.

1979 Norwood Cottage Hospital wards closed, leaving the Outpatient Department only. Croydon Council approved private housing redevelopment plans for the Paddock; demolition started of buildings in Westow Street and in the interior of the Triangle. Crystal Palace Darby & Joan Club closed. David Greigs and Jackson & Son (Drapers) closed. Crystal Palace Foundation launched.

1980 Express Dairy depot in Triangle closed. Abbey Housing Association redevelopment started on High Level Station site.

1981 Dulwich Upper Wood Nature Park in Farquhar Road proposed. Proposals for improvements to Norwood Grove mansion, former home of the Nettlefold family. UNACC social centre opened in St Aubyn's Hall.

1982 Fire destroyed Christ Church, Gipsy Hill, but spared the Church Hall. Vestry and tower, although damaged, still stand. Second edition of *The Phoenix Suburb*.

1983 Gas mains replacement around the Triangle caused traffic disruption; many local traders badly affected. Successful campaign by local people sped up the operation.

1984 'Alley Arts': Gipsy Hill Co-op Workshop set up in premises at the end of Paddock Gardens in the heart of what is left of the original Triangle interior. Local artists and craftspeople have space for producing paintings, portraits, pottery, sculpture, fine joinery, cabinet work, and leather goods; providing opportunities and encouragement to young unemployed.

1985 'Norwood Heights' complex in Westow Street opened: it includes the 'Safeway' supermarket, Salvation Army premises and the Phoenix Community Centre. The only remaining portion of the structure of the original 'White Hart' was demolished. 'Dulwich Upper Wood' opened. UNIT ('Upper Norwood Improvement Team') under the chairmanship of Bernard Weatherill MP began its efforts to revitalise the area.

1986 Adult Training Centre built on the site of the old High Level Crystal Palace Station. Tesco supermarket closed. More high density housing along the Crystal Palace Parade. Traffic chaos caused by installation of new water main along Church Road. Bromley published proposals for the future of the Crystal Palace site, including improvement of the park landscaping and furniture and a recreation centre as well as a hotel on the Palace site. The 50th anniversary of the Crystal Palace Fire marked by a publication: *'Fire!'*, by a CPF event and a BBC programme. UNIT proposed an extension of the Underground to Crystal Palace. *'Palace of the People'*, by Graham Reeves published. Extension of Church Road Conservation Area originally designated in 1974.

1987 Environmental improvements for the Triangle announced by Croydon, including paving, trees and street furniture. Controversy over plans for a hotel on the Palace site. Plans for the extension of the 'Queen's Hotel'. The centenary of St Johns Church marked by a number of local events. *'Camille Pissarro at the Crystal Palace'* published by its author Nicholas Reed. A meeting at 'Queen's Hotel' about the Triangle organised by UNIT. Battle for the preservation of 'The Hollies'. North Area Advisory Panel set up by Croydon for the Norwood area. Hurricane caused damage to many of the area's fine trees. New Christ Church rededicated.

1988 'The Hollies' site redeveloped. Norwood Grove listed by English Heritage. 'Kwik Save' supermarket opens premises on Westow Hill. The Triangle proposed first by CPTCA, then by UNIT as a Conservation Area. Woolworths store burns down. Petition for its restoration. Launch of first edition of this book with unveiling of local map jointly sponsored by Safeways and the publishers.

1989 The Triangle declared a Conservation Area by Croydon. Facade of old Sorting Office replaced by 'Fun Junction'; the yellow sign of Kebab King shrieks from the upper stories of Westow Hill. What *were* the planners up to? Still we are told Woolworths will be rebuilt. First edition of *Crystal Palace/Norwood Heights* sold out!

Brock's Benefit

Beyond the arch-topped windows
Chains of electric lights
Trace out in growing dusk
The terraces and steps,
The gardens, lakes and fountains.

The great glass Palace empties:
Folks gather in the expectant gloom.
Up there on the balcony, the 'Nobs'.
I squeeze Dad's hand, he squeezes back.

In sky above great candelabras
Suddenly light themselves:
Red. Blue. Silver. Gold . . .
And, crackling, disappear.

A thousand perfect pleasures
Reflected in Palace walls:
Brief illuminations never quite explained
Flash on a mass of people
On terrace, step and slope.

I do not want the magnificence to die,
Ever to fade. I do not want to leave.
I want to stay and watch for ever
That fleeting absolute beauty
Emulating stars and flowers, feathers, fountains.

At the Finale:
Chains of firework lights
Trace out 'God Save Our King & Queen'
But do not stir my heart to patriotic flights.
My love is for that former loveliness
Not tethered to this earth, this time, these growing pains.

Brian Dann

View over Woodland Valley

This is the valley that I have seen for the past 20 years from our kitchen, full of trees – poplars, ash, black poplars, chestnut, silver birch, pine and many fruit trees. A glorious view, especially for London. In summer, swifts scream past our bedroom windows as they feed on the wing.

The view is punctuated now by the BBC TV mast, a strange, elegant, winking, blinking finger of steel pointing skywards. For 80 years the Crystal Palace must have dominated the skyline until the eye-searing night when it went up in flames. I try to imagine how it towered above the trees and houses. It was enormous. It must have been a wonderful sight, especially in the evenings when all that glass sent back flashing reflections of the setting sun.

The scene continues to change. Paxton School, (originally Woodland Road School), a massive old London School Board building, constructed in 1886 with purplish-red bricks and fine 'Pont Street Dutch' gables, was demolished in the 1970s and another red brick Victorian building – the Ravenstone Hotel – was revealed on the other side of the valley. But not for long. continued–

31

Soon fires were burning in its garden and we watched it come down. A block of flats replaced it, pretty well screened by trees. The trees along the skyline provide a delicate and constantly changing edge to the world from the window. Over the years I have watched two beeches performing graceful arabesques as they emerge above the general level. There were two enormous black poplars in a neighbour's garden – homes for many birds, including an owl. But one was rotten and had to come down, and the other was fiercely pollarded. In a nearer garden three Lombardy poplars swayed and flourished. A storm blew one down, and then for a time there were two. Then one of those became dangerous and had to be cut, and the survivor was 'topped' rather crudely. This spring it is sprouting as blithely as ever.

The seasons cause a multitude of changes in shapes and colours, as does the weather. Although spring, summer and autumn sunshine make colours and contrasts brilliant, the view I almost prefer is in winter, when clouds rush past, or pile up, the damp air makes colours rich, and roofs are shiny with rain. AH

◀ Paxton School and poplars in Autumn

▲ Paxton School through window in Summer

▶ View down garden in snow

◀ Paxton School from the Ravenstone Hotel

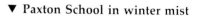
▼ Paxton School in winter mist

◄ Door into St Andrew's Church from Church Road

We discovered this door in Church Road quite soon after we came to live in Norwood. For how long would anything so rich with age escape notice and be thrown away and replaced with something new and serviceable and smart? That wonderful blistered paint, with the elegant lettering curving with its distortions, the definitely ecclesiastical brown old scuffed door, and even the silted up step all made us hold our breath every time we passed it. The inevitable happened: one day there was a door from somebody's catalogue, and the space above it cemented in. And someone had broken up the blistered paint and heaved the old door on to a skip without so much as a thought for its 100 years. AH

RECOLLECTIONS

Audrey Hammond

The first memory I have of coming to Crystal Palace was of getting off a bus at the Parade in 1946 – I remember the railings distinctly – and my mother asking a policeman if this was Crystal Palace. 'Yes, ma'am!' he said, 'have a good time!' I heard my mother say to herself: 'What cheek!'

The next time was in November 1951 when I was a student at Bromley College of Art. Another student and I set out from Bromley for a walk. We walked and talked as students will, unaware of the miles, through Beckenham and Penge, along Thicket Road and up Anerley Hill. Of course, I knew nothing of those names then, and remember little of the walk except for an indelible memory of looking up Palace Road – terrace houses on either side, angles of roofs and hundreds of smoking chimney pots: all greys and blues and mauves, and the red sun setting somewhere at the end of it, somewhere over Belvedere Road. We took a 227 bus back to Bromley.

Before we were married, my husband Martin and I used to cycle up and down the hills of Crystal Palace and along the quiet roads lined with huge trees and

big old houses, and think that we would like to live there.

Later when Martin became a post-graduate student at the Royal College of Art, we had to live within cycling distance of South Kensington, so that he could get to college. If one had to live near London, Crystal Palace seemed about the best place. It had an atmosphere left over perhaps from another, quieter age. In the 1950s it was much the same as it had been in the 1930s, even the 1920s, even, possibly, in a few places the same as before the First World War.

Finding anywhere to live was as difficult then as it is now, but eventually we did find a flat – a chilly but roomy semi-basement with a large garden on the corner of Hamlet and Belvedere Roads. We moved there in 1956 with our first two children. We had very little money, like most people around Anerley. I once asked the greengrocer at our Hamlet shops if she would sell me half a pound of potatoes. She was perfectly happy to. I said 'Mrs Jones, you will never make a fortune.' She replied, 'No, but as long as I make a living. . . .' One evening I found I had just run out of flour, essential for our supper. Since I was very pregnant, getting the children coated-and-hatted and down to the shop before it closed was out of the question. So I made use of our recently acquired telephone and asked the grocer if by any chance there was a customer in his shop who lived in our road and who wouldn't mind bringing it. The dear man got on his bike and brought it to me himself.

By our gate, outside our kitchen window, there was a street-lamp – a gas one. A little man in a black suit and a cap came regularly on his bicycle to polish the glass and to replace the mantle when necessary. We all used to watch – fascinated.

Crystal Palace Park

We discovered the Crystal Palace Park which was overgrown and jungly in those days. The Zoo – with its baby animals and the donkey and its goats which ate one's shopping (even the paper bags) – was a delight.

Many of the big old houses were decaying gently, like their elderly owners. The gardens were overgrown, old roses grew to tremendous heights, shrubs flourished, weeds and daisies abounded and birds found paradise. Without staff and maintenance and in some cases, owners, many Victorian mansions showed cracks and missing slates. Some were taken over as half-way houses or suchlike; many were turned rather amateurishly into flats. Some were left empty waiting for something to happen.

While other suburbs were beginning to be redeveloped – their history hastily and thoughtlessly destroyed and usually replaced with unbelievably unin-

teresting brick or concrete structures, countless flats squashed on to small sites, office blocks, supermarkets and multi-storey carparks – somehow Crystal Palace still seemed to be forgotten. We hardly realised this of course, although the occasional visit to Croydon (by contrast so characterless and inhuman in its new style) shocked and horrified us, and sent us thankfully back to our haven. Few people had cars so the roads here were still quiet and some were still 'unmade' – we could walk to the Horniman Museum along a good dirt road. There were woods and a few noble mansions to pass and outside one house there was a mounting block for the children to climb on. We explored overgrown gardens on some of our walks, picked blackberries and rummaged undisturbed while the children climbed trees or made camps in the undergrowth. We pushed prams or push-chairs accompanied by the older children, now on trikes or bikes, on long expeditions, and always there were hills.

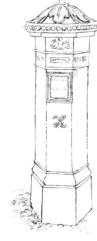

Victorian pillar box as invented by Anthony Trollope. This one is on Sydenham Hill but there is another in Belvedere Road.

Sometimes we went 'up the hill' to the Triangle for special shopping – wholefoods from the pale-haired lady at Culpeppers, cheese cut on a marble slab at Cullens, with its rows of glass-topped biscuit tins, children's clothes at Maney & Cummings, shoes at Gibberds or materials for sheets or pillow-cases from the Material Mart, or to browse in Collins' bookshop, or buy camping gear from Crystal Palace Camping, or anoraks from Jacatex, or to poke round the junk-shops, which varied from 'almost antiques' to absolute junk. Often we ended up at the Library, or Ken Holly's 'The Square Deal', and invariably met or made friends in those places.

Windows over Jacatex, Westow Hill

One of my most vivid and happiest memories is of the walk taking the children from our flat to Mrs Carrick's playgroup in Palace Grove. On lazy, hot summer afternoons we crossed the shady square into Fox Hill, where two dogs from the lattice-windowed cottage on the leafy corner always rushed to the fence, barking. Then in blissful sunshine we passed old sheds – black paint blistering, leaning under their weight of Russian vine and a thousand bees. Onwards, past someone's kitchen garden, the sandy soil at the edge of the road sifting through our sandals, the scent from masses of shoulder-high roses in the front garden of No 45 wafting across to us as we turned into bumpy, rutty, lovely Palace Grove and made our way to Mrs Carrick's welcome, and her home: a house

much battered by other peoples' children!

Having small children, one soon makes friends among their friends' parents. We found other artists and musicians among the people in Crystal Palace. By then we had four children so I had little time for painting. However I continued to draw constantly, mostly the family. Sometimes I worked on local views. If I had then any idea of how valuable these drawings could be as records of a disappearing age, I would have tried to make many more. For we had the 'Charcoal Burner's' Cottage round the corner at the foot of Fox Hill, 'Norbury Lodge' at its top, with a beautiful south-sloping garden glimpsed through the arched gateway in its wall, and opposite a villa with a great monkey-puzzle tree in the garden, 'Castle Hill', 'Walden House', 'The Tyrol', 'Ly-ee Moon' and 'Home-lands' in Church Road, and many more. Now they are all gone and forgotten.

Although traffic problems were then considered to be serious, they were nothing compared to the present congestion in Westow Hill, Westow Street and Church Road. Consequently it was still pleasant to walk around the Triangle on a sunny Saturday or Sunday morning, and enjoy its village atmosphere.

We looked up mysterious Dickensian passages and glimpsed gardens with fruit trees bathed in sunlight. We explored cobbled alleys and found lace-curtained Victorian cottages with sea-shell decorated walls and climbing roses in their tiny gardens. And further inside the Triangle we found a sun-gathering field in front of a row of cottages. When we first knew it, the Paddock was neatly laid out as allotments. Cabbages, beans and brussels sprouts flourished, but later it became a wilderness: the silver birches around the edge burgeoned into mature trees, the *Buddleia* butterfly bushes reached

amazing heights, the grasses grew soft and long each year, patches of red sorrel spread. We couldn't think why the gardeners from the cottages had abandoned their vegetables. Later we learned that Croydon Council had told them to stop cultivating 'because redevelopment was imminent'. Yet it was many years before the bulldozers finally destroyed the Paddock. In the meantime cats stalked mice or small boys stalked each other, occasionally the Community Association held an Arts Festival, but most of the time Nature had it to herself.

We found another place where a windmill had stood, and a cobbled lane entrance next to the 'Royal Albert', with some very early 19th-century cottages to one side which could well have belonged to the mill. Other cobbled lanes led into a large cobbled yard, surrounded with tumbledown buildings which backed on to the Paddock. These, we found, had been stables for the cab horses which plied for hire in the heyday of the Palace. A larger building in the yard had housed members of the menagerie when

there were a Zoo and Circus at the Palace. On the Paddock side of this building was a corner stone beautifully cut with the letters *WR 1824* which showed that it had been there a long time before the Palace had ever been thought of.

Paddock Passage (1969)

Over the doorway one could see in faint lettering the painted sign 'VULCAN MOTOR CAR & COACH COMPANY', so it had changed uses many times without anyone feeling the need to replace it with a more modern structure. When we found it, and until it was finally demolished, it was used as a laundry.

At this time there were still three Victorian churches in the Triangle, one in each of the roads. Now there is only what used to be St Andrews Presbyterian Church, now the Greek Orthodox Church of St Constantine and St Helen. It seems strange to think that there was a large stone church where 'Kwik Save' now stands – and there were weddings there on Saturday afternoons. Many shopfronts had settled into a sort of comfortable existence with their facades and lettering only a little worn and faded. One assumed that other people, too, looked at and guarded such treasures – but how precarious such permanence, how callous the eye of new owners, as with one slosh of purple paint the gold-and-green three-dimensional name **GARNHAM** could be wiped out!

One wet day while shopping with the children around the Triangle, we heard a terrific clatter. Round the corner by the 'Hollybush' came a strange procession: a young man daubed in mud and paint was being dragged along in a dustbin on wheels by other young men. All were got up in colourful rags and ink. They were laughing and shouting and banging dustbin lids. These lads were all apprentices at Stephens Printers in Belvedere Road and they were celebrating the end of their apprenticeship – a custom going back hundreds of years. The firm was a very large one and employed many men. The barber in Church Road was kept in business by the printers even when long hair for men was the fashion (because of the danger of getting their hair caught up in the machinery). The barbers closed

when Stephens did!

Mr Stephens lived at 155 Auckland Road, where he kept his Stephens veteran motor-car in a large motor-house in his garden. His father had been one of the earliest car-makers in Britain, and Mr Stephens himself would often be seen at the wheel of his rare 1898 Stephens car; he always took part in the veteran car rallies at Crystal Palace and in the London to Brighton run.

The television mast was built. We could see tiny figures of men working on it as it rose higher and higher. A gigantic Sports Centre was built in 1964 in the Crystal Palace grounds. Although the Sports Centre was designed as a national and international competition and training centre, the director set Sunday mornings aside as family time, so our children learned to swim there on our Sunday outings, and we all had the opportunity to meet yet more friends! Paxton was turned around to face down towards the Park and away from the ruins of his Palace.

As it became more difficult to get around with the family on bicycles, we acquired a car – first a little green Austin 10, with a peak, rather like a cloth cap, then a 1928 Alvis saloon. And later, as I took on a bit of teaching, we bought a second Alvis. It never occurred to us to buy anything but old cars; they were beautiful, strong, easy for us to maintain, and cheap to buy and to run.

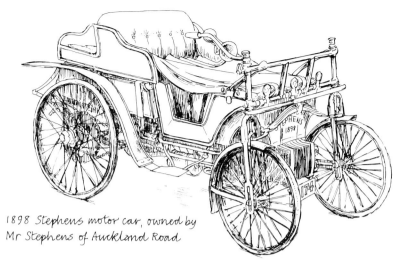

1898 Stephens motor car, owned by Mr Stephens of Auckland Road

In 1965 our landlord sold two-thirds of our garden and into that small space were crammed *three* houses (all mod. con.). They bulldozed the garden while the enormous cherry tree in it was in full fruit. The burning cherries made it smell as though all the neighbourhood was jam-making. Although the flat had seemed roomy enough when we had a garden of grass and trees, our home now seemed cramped indeed. We needed a

bigger house and a larger garden. We were lucky to find a suitable house in Gipsy Hill: just a bit bigger than we had intended, and for a price which we could not really afford, but that is usually the way. . . .

The children had to leave Anerley Mixed Infants and Juniors, but fairly soon settled at Paxton School, which we could see from our new kitchen

window. In spite of now living on a main road, we found the atmosphere much the same; after all we had only moved 'over the hill'. There was a row of shops in Gipsy Hill which could supply almost all needs. Tony, our marvellous milkman, gave us a cheery

welcome when we moved in and still delivers our milk as efficiently as ever 20 years later. And Mrs Bellars the lollipop lady only retired in 1985 after 19 years of seeing the schoolchildren across the road.

Our next door neighbour Mrs Turton, who was in her eighties, had lived in the same house nearly all her life. She did her washing outside her back door using a galvanised tub and a washboard – much to our children's amazement. Our boys used to fire their pea-shooters from the upstairs window at the upturned tub, getting a rewarding 'ping' from it. We acquired a cat, two rabbits, a guinea-pig and a Labrador dog – all great characters.

* * *

One day, walking up Anerley Hill with the dog, thinking about the headlines in the local paper:

'TRIANGLE TO BE COMPLETELY REDEVELOPED' – I could only feel: 'What thoughtlessness, what a tragic end to a London village which many people, myself included, regarded as a familiar homeplace'. At that moment many of my own thoughts about the place seemed to come together.

My own experience with teaching pre-school children, secondary school children and adults had shown me how enjoyable and therapeutic arts and crafts were for so many people – why not an Arts Centre inside the Triangle on the lines of the Birmingham Family Arts Centre? And why not a centre for all sorts of allied activities and also for the essential amenities of the community?

There were many old buildings which could be used: it would be unnecessary to build many new ones, save to link or modify existing structures, in the same way that the famous Kettle's Yard Centre in Cambridge had been created. Since I first heard its originator, Jim Ede, describe it on the radio I had been fascinated by this lovely centre for the arts: paintings, sculpture and music, which was at the same time a home full of other found and collected objects of beauty and interest. How perfectly, how sensitively Jim Ede had restored his old cottages to make a restful haven for students or anyone else to escape the hassle and racket of everyday life, and restore themselves in these surroundings, conceived and maintained in his delightful and tranquil taste.

Could not the Kettle's Yard restrained, sensitive and subtle style of restoration be combined with the construction of a Family Arts and Activities Centre within the Triangle – with cafes, restaurants, cinema, even a theatre – ideas kept coming. The lanes between the shops in Westow Hill, Westow Street, and Church Road would all lead into the 14 acres of the Triangle interior. The shops would flourish again, the Civic Trust might contribute design advice as they had done at Blackheath, to keep the character of the shopfronts, and make the whole place as attractive to tourists as it would be to residents.

Nowadays, with the example of Covent Garden, (and the GLC, then a reformed poacher, patting itself on the back for initiating it!), it doesn't seem so impossible. Then, I suppose, it sounded wildly cranky. The newspaper article which had sparked off this chain of thought contained a reference to the local Chamber of Commerce, so I found the Mrs Dolling, who chaired it, (and who ran, and still does, a café on the Parade). She suggested that I took my ideas to the local newspaper, the *Norwood News*, which had its offices at the corner of Belvedere Road. A reporter made a story out of my ideas.

The best thing to come out of that was a letter from a reader who congratulated me for 'the first human and imaginative idea for the Triangle yet'. That was the beginning of a long friendship with Mike Conrad, the graphic designer and his family. It is Mike who has designed this book and who has made it look so fine.

Cobbled lane into the paddock, from Westow Hill

Then I had to begin writing my ideas down in the form of an article and I approached Mrs Voss the editor of the *Norwood Review*, the magazine of the local amenity group, the Norwood Society, about whose existence I was just learning. She was enthusiastic and delighted to publish my article, which was called 'A Plan for the Triangle'. I had been introduced to Mimi Irving who was interested in the uses to which old buildings could be put, and in 'causes' generally. Together we were asked to a meeting of the Norwood Society to talk about my ideas and we were invited to join the society. However I was disappointed when, after an initially favourable response from the floor, no mention was ever made again of my suggestions for the Triangle at subsequent meetings. Perhaps the idea was too novel and too far outside their normal terms of reference.

It was evident that if anything was to be done, it would have to

Kettles Yard, Cambridge

be through other channels. I had heard about a Community Association in Lymington, which ran many arts activities and as my concept of an Arts Centre was one which would involve the whole community, perhaps a Community Association would be more appropriate. Mimi and I drew up a list of all the local people involved in churches, societies and activity groups or who ran local businesses, schools and so forth. We invited them to my house to see first a show of slides of the area taken by my husband Martin. These illustrated the special character of the area. We then heard a talk by Mr Parry, secretary of the National Federation of Community Associations, on how to set up a Community Association. There was much interest in the idea and consequently a steering committee was set up then and there.

Between September and December 1969, most of the business of setting up our particular Association was thrashed out, including our rather long-winded name: the Crystal Palace Triangle Community Association (CPTCA). We were ready to be formally constituted in January 1970, just in time for our ideas to be incorporated in an exhibition of plans and suggestions for the Triangle, organised by the Norwood Society in an empty shop in Westow Hill.

The history of the CPTCA needs a book to itself, but a page or so will have to suffice here. With 20 or more energetic people organising the sorts of events they would like to see going on in the proposed Arts Centre – drama, music, poetry, chess, dance, with rambles, camping and pot-holing thrown in for good measure – there was soon a large membership. Without a centre, activities were held in hired halls, in the open, or in members' own homes. Oliver and Gunnvor Stallybrass hosted literally hundreds of events at their home on Westwood Hill – from quiet chess matches to orchestral concerts.

At one of our first children's events – a 'playday' involving over 50 children – a father brought his two children and then stayed all day to help. Then, at our first Kaleidoscope (an evening event of music, playlets, poetry etc. where members were invited to provide their own entertainment– and food!), he revealed himself as a dedicated poet. This was Brian Dann, who has been deeply involved with CPTCA ever since, compèring the Kaleidoscopes with the most perfect and sensitive touch, providing poems for every occasion, in fact *being* poetry in the Triangle – our 'resident poet'.

There were activities for children, events for old people and Festivals, including one a week long commemorating the 120th anniversary of the opening of Crystal Palace in 1854 on Norwood Heights. In this last every local organisation was very much involved. Ian Hempstead and I screen-printed hundreds of colourful posters which kindly shopkeepers displayed in their windows and so brightened the Triangle. And there were crises to cope with – the dreaded GLC Road Plan – and the scare when the then GLC threatened a Disneyland type of leisure centre on the Crystal Palace site (the CPTCA countered with a plan for an educational farm). The Crystal Palace Forum was set up but sadly came to nothing. We added our voice to that of the Norwood Society in asking for a more sympathetic approach from local planning authorities for the visual qualities and underlying character of the Triangle area.

But the hardest and most disappointing part was trying to stem the growing tide of development, and stop the destruction of old buildings which held the character of the area. One night in 1982 Christ Church burned to the ground: another fine building and local landmark was added to the list of those destroyed in one way or another. Over and over again appeals to councils to prevent the

loss of an important shopfront, house or open space seemed to fall on deaf ears. We soon learned which of our five councils were sympathetic to conservation, and which were not! We learned about 'Listed Buildings', 'Grades 1, 2, and 3', and 'Conservation Areas', and how unless a historic area was 'Designated', especially one of more recent historical interest like the Triangle, there was no hope of protection.

We did all that we could to add our weight of opinion to the voice of the older amenity group, the Norwood Society, with its broader geographical interests, in an effort to stem the tide of demolition and thoughtless redevelopment. Lambeth set up the Westow Hill General Improvement Area (after prompting by the CPTCA). Conservation areas did appear: Gipsy Hill in Lambeth, Belvedere Road/Fox Hill in Bromley, Harold Road and Church Road in Croydon, but the Triangle was left out. Although Croydon's Urban Design Group pressed its importance, the Department of the Environment refused to recognise it as an area of intrinsic historical and visual value worth designating. So, without that vital protection old buildings of character

have been destroyed, spaces filled with unsuitable development and shopfronts lost. Yet within a few years Victorian buildings and areas with a group character and value will be recognised as worth conserving. Will there be many left anywhere to conserve?

It was in order to draw attention to the visual qualities of the Triangle, its value as a recognisable entity for its community and the need for conservation that I started making pictures of views which seemed to show strongly the character of the area. The first two were the 'Hollybush' and the 'White Hart'. The latter was published in the *Evening Standard* to illustrate an article about the CPTCA's ideas for reviving the Triangle. Other drawings followed: Inside the Triangle, Haynes Lane, Ken Holly's shop and 'Hilltop'. All six were produced as a set of prints, also on cards and stationery, and sold in aid of CPTCA funds. They have sold steadily ever since. But there seemed less time for drawing than ever – our growing family, my part-time teaching and my great involvement with CPTCA activities consumed all of my time. So records lapsed until Croydon Council's crucial decision to sell

The White Hart, Crystal Palace.

The Paddock

Audrey Hammond

the land containing the Paddock, the Laundry, the stables and the cottages inside the Triangle to developers shocked me into making a series of pictures in the lovely late summer and autumn of 1979, showing these places for the last time.

These pictures were shown in the Library in an exhibition called 'The Vanishing Triangle'. It caused a flurry of local interest, but by then it was too late, the bulldozers soon laid waste the whole area, and a housing development of uninspiring design quickly appeared in the heart of the Triangle.

When most of the family had grown and flown I continued drawing and recording, either in my VW Camper (our Alvises eventually went to enthusiasts) or at kindly loaned windows or outside, often very cold. If I am drawing out on the street many people stop to discuss with me the subject of the picture. If it is a building about to be demolished there is usually disgust expressed that 'they' could allow it. Children are always interested and are often aware that there is something special about the old house or shop being drawn. The figures in the pictures are always portraits – fleeting glimpses retained in the memory or in thumbnail sketches round the borders. Somebody once told me they recognised their cat in a painting!

Some people tell me that I make Crystal Palace look more attractive than it really is. But I only depict what is there. If the pictures help people to look again at the buildings, they may find for themselves that Crystal Palace is more attractive than they thought. People say to me: 'But you always leave out the litter'. Of course. The sight of litter all over the streets (however historic) can make all the difference between a cared-for, attractive looking place and what is almost a slum. It is not only a reflection on the street-cleaning care by the Council, but also on

the attitude of local people. It is not difficult to take one's wrappers, sweet papers and take-away cartons home or put them in a bin, and to teach one's children to do the same. Yet so many seem unaware that their scrap of paper adds to the drifts of litter about the streets and contributes to making their own locality look the sort of place they would not like to live in themselves. So I usually leave the litter out and hope that the pictures will reveal not only details and views previously unnoticed by the viewer, but also show how good their place could look if cared for a little more.

I do not leave out signs, street furniture and road markings. I feel these are now part of the business of life in a town and, therefore, have become part of the structure. They have a pattern and a quality of their own that quite often comes from being well-designed for their purpose. (Not always: I have in mind some particularly hideous concrete lamp posts!) I *do* succumb to the temptation to reconvert buildings, or parts of buildings to their original state, especially when a window, for instance, has recently been 'modernised'.

*   *   *

People also ask: 'Why such enthusiasm?' I sometimes wonder

myself. The first part of these recollections explains my initial attraction to this place, but we have lived here only for 30 years, so my loyalty can hardly be compared to those who have lived here for a lifetime, and their parents before them.

The only connection that I had been aware of was that my grand-parents on my father's side had lived in Thornton Heath for their entire married life from 1906 onwards. But it now seems that I have closer connections with the area than I could possibly have imagined. While researching the history of the growth of Norwood from forest to village, I re-read Alan Warwick's *The Phoenix Suburb* and my attention was caught by the name of the first parson of All Saints' Church: Rev. Edmund Harden. Since my grandmother's maiden name was also Harden I could not help feeling a certain excitement as I searched for an old family Bible inherited from my father. Sure enough, on the flyleaf, written in several different hands were set out several generations of Hardens, beginning with Nathaniel, born in 1763, who died and was buried in Norwood in 1842. Of his three surviving sons, Nathaniel, Philip and Edmund, the first and eldest was my great-great-grandfather and the youngest, Edmund, it seems was first Curate and then Vicar of All Saints' until his death at the age of 60 (from, according to Alan Warwick, hurrying to a wedding feast and eating too much ice- [or was it rice-?] pudding) on May 29 1856.

It is delightful to imagine my great-great-uncle living in the Vicarage in Church Road and strolling to his new church along that country lane with his father and brothers and his own large family. Or perhaps walking or riding in other directions to visit his parishioners in the Triangle then? Did they find the construction of the Crystal Palace an exciting new development or an incursion into the quiet life of the

country village? Since making this discovery I have learnt many more facts about the Harden family who continued to live in South London – Streatham and Blackheath – although my grandmother was born in Australia. Among other papers is the diary kept by her mother, my great-grandmother, of the three-month long voyage by sailing ship with her three small sons when she went to join her husband Theodore Harden there. It would be interesting to know why this branch of the family returned to the Norwood area. At any rate they returned to the family, for my grandparents were married in 1906 at St Andrew's, Streatham, by the Rev. Henry Harden, Edmund Harden's son, who was then 78!

So now I have another trail to follow – to trace this part of the family's connections with Norwood – where they all lived, where they worked, who they married and where their descendants are now. So, why the enthusiasm? Perhaps it is race-memory!

*   *   *

There are still dozens of views and shops and hundreds of indi-

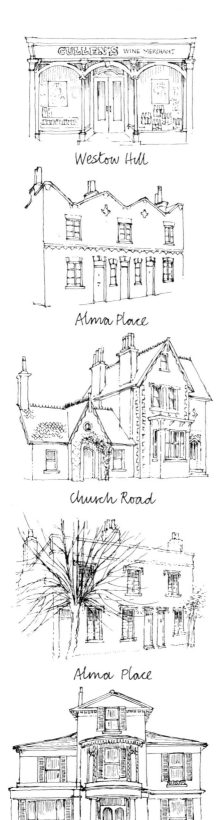

Westow Hill

Alma Place

Church Road

Alma Place

Church Road

vidual houses I would like to have included in this book. (I could make a whole book of the trees of Norwood alone!) So why publish if my work is incomplete? Because we need to show to a larger audience the views, houses and shops and trees that hold the character and atmosphere of this particular and unique part of London before it is entirely gone and forgotten.

Where once change went on slowly, at a pace people could cope with, now familiar surroundings disappear and are replaced at dizzying speed with brash new buildings. And the new usually means 'Econo-Architecture': the cheapest materials, fastest building methods, most complete infill of land and least time, thought and money spent on design. There are notable exceptions: the new Norwood Heights shopping centre in Westow Street has been carefully and imaginatively designed to blend with the rest of the street – but who will protect the comfortable row of old shops opposite, to which it relates?

There is also the other kind of change – an insidious change that catches one unawares. One suddenly realises that a shop or other building has lost its character and style by a misguided revamping under the name of restoration. Restoration can involve a sensitive understanding of the qualities which give a building its character, so that materials used in any reconstructions made, retain the style, proportions and essential quality of the original. Unfortunately there are many examples in Crystal Palace where this is not the case, and where the vogue for hacking appearances about is all the more sad as many places have hung on in their original state for so long – almost long enough, one would think, to benefit from all the publicity in the media on conservation and what 'looks right'. We must not forget it was his horror and indignation at the 'restoration' of Tewkesbury Abbey by Sir

Gilbert Scott that provoked William Morris to found the Society for the Protection of Ancient Buildings!

Finally, there is the ever-spreading rash of multinational 'fast food' shops which look the same everywhere, making Bangkok and Brighton look equally anonymous. However useful they are at saving, or preventing, people from cooking fresh food, they are as boring to draw as to look at.

*   *   *

Making pictures is a very personal business for the artist; it is a means of expressing feelings about some thing or things which move him or her especially. For the viewers there is the pleasure and satisfaction of seeing pictures which express for them visually and emotionally their own feelings about a subject; or which help them to see truths that they felt hazy about – or just unsure of; or which show them aspects of a subject about which they were previously unaware. Such are the possibilities and revelations which the artist can communicate to his audience, whether or not they are familiar with the subject.

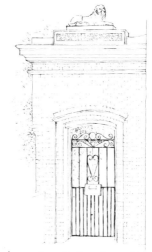

Side gate, Belvedere Road

When both artist and audience are held by the same ties of affection, loyalty and concern to the subject of the pictures, which happens to be a place, this place, their own place, Crystal Palace, Upper Norwood, then there is a further rapport, a sort of mutual understanding. Even for people for whom pictures would not always rate much there is the delight of recognition, familiarity and revelation. There is reassurance too, because someone else has cared enough to make pictures of what is part of their past and background, or a living and discoverable present.

▲ **Christmas cards:**
Snow in the moonlight
Crystal Palace Park in snow
Audrey and Martin Hammond delight their friends with their own original Christmas cards, taking it in turns each year to design and make the Hammond card. These two lino-prints were made by Audrey in 1981 and 1983. BD

Boundaries

Bromley, Croydon, Lambeth, Lewisham,
Southwark, Crystal Palace Park:
The fag-end of each London Borough
Where burning issues stub themselves on boundaries.

Walking the littered, lorry-broken paving slabs
I kick a carton emptied of Kentucky Fried
Across the frontier, a line drawn on a map
Between Croydon and Lambeth.

There's no line on the ground.
Ignorance and poverty
Leak across the boundary.

Brian Dann

▲ All Saints' Church

The foundation stone of this church was laid by Lady Carey, wife of Lord Falkland, in 1827. At that time it was intended to be a 'Chapel of Ease' to accommodate the increasingly large numbers of Croydon parishioners then living in the Norwood area. The church was consecrated in 1829 and Edmund Harden MA (qv) was installed as its curate.

In its original form as designed by James Savage it had neither steeple nor tower. It was built in a somewhat pared-down version of the architect's Gothic concept, divested of many details, and in rather poorer quality facing bricks than those originally specified. In the years immediately following its construction the Church Commission must have had cause to regret the parsimony which led to these and similar economies: the cappings of the pillars at three of the corners became detached at various times and damaged the roof. These incidents led to disputes with the architect and the contractors.

The tower and steeple were added in 1841. The church was made a Parish Church in 1845, when Edmund Harden was made its first vicar.

Many local dignitaries, including Admiral Fitzroy and members of the Carey family as well as the Rev. Harden were buried in its graveyard which became the subject of a bizarre dispute in 1869. Details of this are given in Alan Warwick's book 'The Phoenix Suburb'. BD

The tomb of Admiral Fitzroy, All Saints' churchyard

▲ The Old Vicarage, 215–217 Church Road

The Vicarage was built about 1840. It had a splendid garden, laid out about the same time, with many marvellous and unusual trees around it. These included Ash, Lime, Silver Birch, Sycamore, Yew, Holly, Pine, English Oak, Holm Oak, Cedar, Acacia, Mulberry and a Monkey Puzzle tree. It must have been an ideal place for all the various activities that went on in a populous and growing Victorian parish. Its conversion to retirement flats has retained the character of its frontage along Church Road, but many of the trees have gone from the garden from which this view was painted. BD

► The Old House, 112 Church Road, from the garden

A lovely garden with ponies in the stables when this picture was drawn. The fine frontage along Church Road had a beautiful balcony and a glass covered entrance way paved with tiles. The roofed gate echoed the house's tower with its cast-iron decorated ridge. The window openings were decorated with beautiful swagging. In its heyday it must have been quite something, with "a private music room with a hydraulically operated revolving stage, which led through double doors to a ground floor bedroom"! Alas its size and age meant that the costs of maintaining it as a private home became increasingly insupportable. The house suffered some unsuitable modification in the course of an abortive attempt to turn it into a private medical clinic. It is now being more sympathetically restored and converted into retirement flats but at the cost of much of this splendid garden. BD

▶ 'Hilltop', Central Hill

The picture shows 'Hilltop' in its post-war state, after fire-bomb damage had destroyed its top storey. What a fine view Dr Gandy, the Police Surgeon who lived here before the War, must have had from those vanished top floor windows! The house formed a notable landmark at the end of Westow Hill and crowned the top of Central and Gipsy Hills. Dr Gandy and his son are commemorated in the seat incorporated into the wall at the top of Gipsy Hill as part of the Central Hill estate. BD

◀ 124 Church Road

This house was built on the site of a hunting lodge, like so many other large houses in the area ('Kingswood' and 'Norwood Grove' are other examples). With its sloping site there is a lower ground floor reached by a staircase whose soffit incorporated a large display of stuffed birds, appropriate to the house's origins!

No. 124 has been the home of several local dignitaries, and more recently, Ken Russell, the film director.

It is one of several listed buildings in the area: Church Road boasts three, all in a row. Many other attractive Victorian houses can still be seen along its tree-lined length. There are some sad gaps, such as that previously occupied by 'Castle Hill', which stood opposite this house but which was demolished in haste in 1970 before local conservationists could take effective action. It has been replaced by modern flats. Fortunately these gaps and incursions are camouflaged during the summer months by the foliage of Church Road's plentiful trees, so that the general appearance of the road has been kept over the years. BD

◀ Watermen's cottages at top of Belvedere Road

During the last century and long before the Crystal Palace came to be built the 'White Hart' was an extremely popular country pub. It had close connections with Thames watermen, and these houses at the top of Belvedere Road were originally built as almshouses for them. More substantial almshouses still in use are to be found at Penge next to the 'Crooked Billet'. Notice the Regency curved canopies on these still attractive cottages. BD

Audrey Hammond May '76

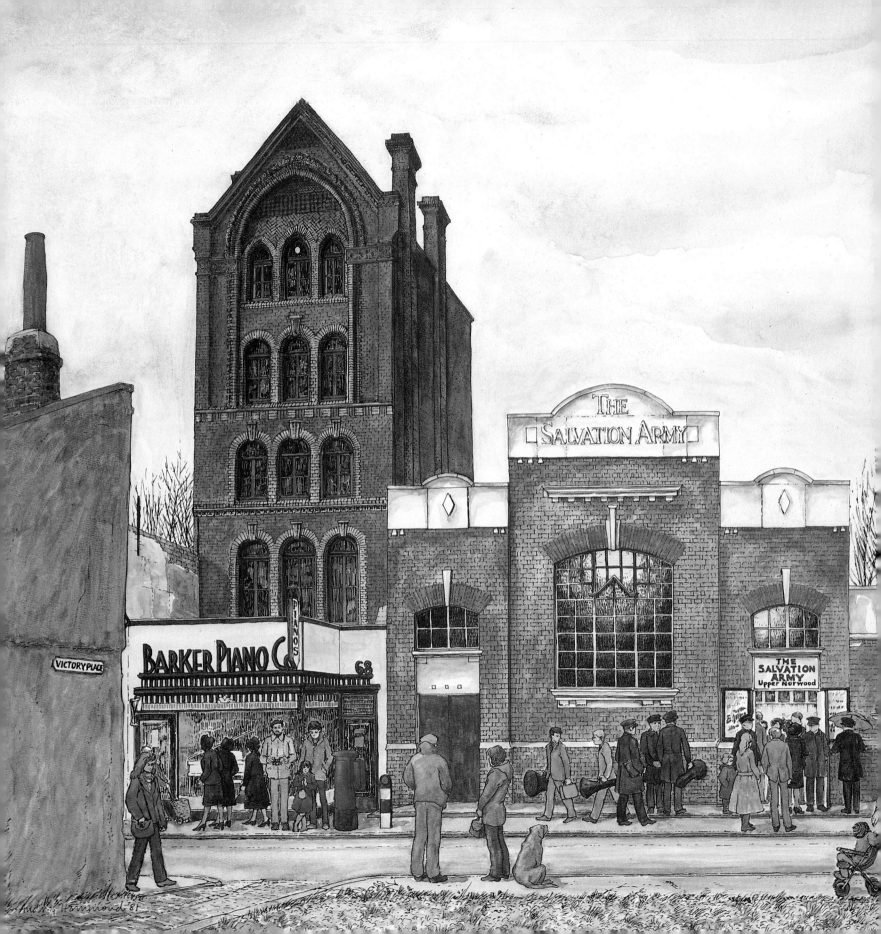

Audrey Hammond

◀ **Westow Street: Salvation Army Hall and Barker's Piano Store**

The Barker's Piano shop shown here stood opposite what is now the 'Picture Palace' shop in Westow Street.

This landmark was originally part of the extensive premises of Evans & Williams (62–8 Westow Street), a very large firm of general drapers. The company had a shop 136 feet long, below which were workrooms in which over fifty needlewomen laboured with busy fingers. The tall building incorporated the staff dining rooms and kitchens, as well as other offices and

workrooms, including an extensive millinery department.

Later it became used as a store for gymnastics equipment before the Barker firm moved here from the church hall at 1 Gipsy Hill. Mr Barker, the son of the firm's founder, lived for some years at 126 Church Road.

The Salvation Army has a long history of association with the area: at one time the old Laundry premises in the Paddock across Westow Street were Salvation Army barracks, before this hall was built in the 1920s. Now this

hall has gone, and the Army has new premises within the 'Norwood Heights' development. BD

▲ **Jackson's, Drapers, Westow St**

In the 1920s Jackson's was the leading Drapers and Haberdashers in the area. It hardly changed over the years. The 'young Mr Jackson' who was approaching retirement in the 1970s still kept it much the same. For many elderly people it was much appreciated as providing the sort of service to which they were used. The shopfront was declared to be 'a Victorian masterpiece' by Croydon's planners, though no thought appears to have been given to the preservation of its interior, unique though this was. BD

◀ **Westow Street: Norwood Heights Shopping Centre**

This interesting and sympathetic new scheme includes the Phoenix Communtiy Centre as well as the Safeways supermarket, shops and Salvation Army hall and was designed by David A Collins of Elsworth Sykes Partnership. Happily the splendid row of trees along the frontage have been preserved.

Unfortunately it appears that the very shops across the road which the new building was designed to blend with are under threat from some who consider them to provide "an indifferent townscape"! BD

▼ **5, 6 and 7 Carberry Road**

These Georgian cottages were demolished in 1979 to make car parking space! In 1978 an enterprising couple would have bought these tiny cottages from Croydon and restored them as one home for themselves. But a vent from the old Laundry next door gushed steam into the back gardens and they were told that there was "no hope of this being removed, or the Laundry going"; The Laundry was demolished in 1979! BD

◄ **Shops and church, east side of Westow Street**

A fine row of old shops, including 'The Picture Palace', 'The Shilling Excursion' and 'Crystal Palace Fine Antiques' which have all been restored to much of their former splendour and contribute to making this one of the most attractive parts of the Triangle. BD

▼ **Workshops behind Westow Street**

A yard of workshops behind Westow Street (through that Dickensian passage). Stone masons and gilders work here now. For nearly forty years, until a few years ago, the cottage at the end was the workshop of Mr Capon, wireworker. AH

▶ **Westow Street: five shops demolished in late 1979**

This row of two-storey shops dates from well before the late 1860's and was demolished to provide the access to the Barratt 'Paxton' estate. These smaller buildings gave a pleasantly human scale to the early Triangle, created in response to the growing needs of the local Gentry. The three- (and in places four-) storey developments which date from the later 1860's, while appropriate to the monumental scale of the Crystal Palace after it had been built, now look rather out of place without the giant and glittering backcloth. Perhaps the earlier two-storey shops and houses with their slate roofs and white stucco are on a scale and colouration more in keeping with the present-day Triangle. BD

© Audrey Hammond '79/83

Bracket above Olga Patisserie

Passage to garden and workshops in Westow street

▲ **Hollybush Stores,**
12-16 Westow Street

This busy hardware shop is now incorporated into one of the remaining two-storey buildings in Westow Street. The shop was originally next to the 'Hollybush' Public House on the other side of the road, hence its name. BD

Clock over opticians in Church Road (1969)

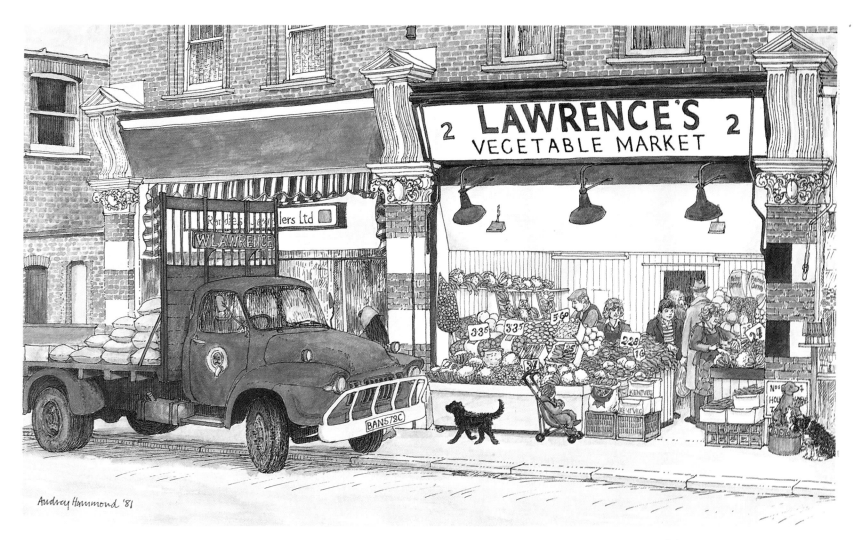

Audrey Hammond '81

▲ Lawrence's Vegetable Market, 2 Hollybush Terrace, Westow Street

One of three Lawrence family shops in the Triangle. The family have had fruit and vegetable shops in the area since 1951 when they came from "over the water". Alfred Lawrence started his business in Westow Hill, then opened shops at 2 Hollybush Terrace, and later at 54 Westow Hill. Three generations of the family have traded in the Triangle and they regret the loss of the old buildings and the village atmosphere that has occurred during their time here. BD

▶ Haynes Lane, off Westow St

This charming terrace of superior artisans' dwellings is in a good state of preservation, happily with most of the original windows and doors still in place. This speaks highly of the quality of work of the original builder, Mr Heynes (qv), after whom the lane was misnamed by Croydon Council. BD

Glass Cut to the Trade.

A very old painted sign in Westow Street

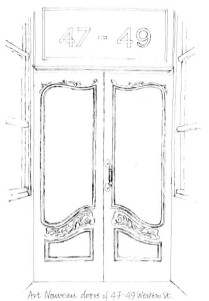

Art Nouveau doors of 47-49 Westow St.

Audrey Hammond '85

► Glass, Butchers, Westow Hill

This handsome shopfront in the middle of Westow Hill was run as an old-fashioned butchers, with sawdust to clean the floor, and a shop window decorated with paper scrolls when the meat was cleared away after the day's trade. It was preserved from insensitive "improvement" by Croydon Council in the nick of time in 1972, after prompting by the CPTCA. Later it was destroyed by a particularly brutal redevelopment and had a brief life as the blank cement face of a night-club, before that was turned into the more acceptable and open face of 'Rickshaws' restaurant. BD

◄ Jacksons, Printers, 55 Westow Street

Printers have worked on this site for over 150 years. Once upon a time 29 people worked here; almost everything was done by hand, though the pride of the shop was at one time to have gas-powered printing machinery. There was a well in the back garden. This is the most perfect example of a Victorian shop still left in the Triangle: a photograph dating from the 1880's shows the exterior looking exactly the same as it did in early 1985!

The shopfront has been lovingly restored by Glyn Peacock as 'The Picture Palace' and the interior, once filled with all the paraphenalia of the letterpress printer, has been turned into a delightful art gallery and framing shop. BD

◄ Olga Patisserie, 40 Westow Street

Continental bread, cakes and confections are sold here. BD

◄ Peters' Fishmonger's Shop: 3 Westow Street

Our own wet fish shop: housed in one of the few remaining two-storey structures which predate the Palace. BD

◄ Upper Norwood Library

This is a rare thing, a Public Library jointly run by two separate London Boroughs: Croydon and Lambeth. I can remember, as a schoolboy, finding it a gloomy and rather unfriendly place which only my great love of books rendered tolerable. Pat Scott, the Chief Librarian, has transformed this place into a lively and useful information centre, with exhibitions and holiday activities for children in their own library. BD

▼ Ken Holly's Antique shop Westow Hill

Known at times as the 'Bird-in-Hand' and later as the 'Square Deal' this shop was piled up to the ceiling with a positive cornucopia of Victorian debris, junk and genuine 'finds'. An entire cabinet was devoted to Crystal Palace memorabilia. BD

▲ Cobbled lane leading into the Paddock

▲ Beardell Street

Just on the left, past the Library Car Park entrance, is our local blacksmith's shop, Gwynn Townsend's, run by a lady blacksmith. Originally the firm was located in Paddock Gardens. Her father from whom she inherited the business was the inventor, among other useful devices, of a special horse-shoe for coping with the steep climbs on every side of the Triangle.

This prospect of London spread out at the bottom of the hill takes one's mind off the sad fact that this steep slope has no handrail for the many old folk who have to toil up and down its narrow pavements, often made more hazardous by thoughtlessly parked cars. BD

Barclays Bank

▲ The Woodman, Westow Hill

The 'Woodman' no longer exists: it used to be where Joanna's wine bar now stands with its distinctive and appropriate frontage in the premises first erected in 1957. But the influence of the 'Woodman' affected the Triangle for many years after its demolition. The name obviously relates to the tree-felling and coppicing activities which were prominent in the Great North Wood which at times extended northwards through Dulwich and Herne Hill and southwards to Croydon and Penge Commons. The inn sign was of a woodman with a bundle of cut branches on his back, accompanied by his dog.

The Woodman of the early 19th century was a comparatively imposing two-storey building with an impressive four-columned portico and a very large cobbled yard behind it, entered through an elegant gateway capable of accomodating the largest stage-coach. This extensive yard included cottages for ostlers and servants, stabling and along one side of the hotel an overhead glazed canopy to shield dismounting passengers from the rigours of the weather. There were tea-gardens, two skittle alleys (one for the gentry) and it was said that the top of the Woodman's doorstep was level with the cross on the top of St Paul's cathedral which in those days was directly visible from the site.

All that remains of this building is the yard which is the same shape on modern maps as in the 1840's, although the pub was rebuilt as a serious drinking place in 1876. The yard was used for the horse cabs which plied for hire until the advent of the motor car. Contemporary photographs show a rather undistinguished but solid three-storey building which matched the shop frontages on either side.

The reason given by the brewers Watney Coombe Reid for the closing of the pub was decline of trade and the reason for the present building line was given as 'road widening'.

The large cobbled yard that remains was at one time surrounded by tumbledown buildings which backed on the the Paddock. These had been stables for the cab horses in the heyday of the Crystal Palace, and a larger building in the group had housed animals from the menagerie when there was a Zoo and Circus at the Palace. It dated from a long time before the Palace and had changed uses many times: at one time it had been the Salvation Army barracks; in the years before it was demolished it formed the premises of a Laundry. BD

▲ The Egg Stall, Westow Hill.

◀ The 'Royal Albert'

Though this doesn't seem a very prepossessing pub from the outside, compared with the magnificence of the 'Cambridge', say, its interior has been transformed by the splendid collection of jugs and pottery which the landlord and his wife have assembled through the years. The pub is a very welcoming one, with lots of laughter and singing! The 'Egg Stall' next door owed its rather 'ad hoc' appearance to the fact that it is based on the sole remaining market stall in the area. This, with its iron-tyred wheels and its steel leaf-springs was the remnant of a once bustling street market which had been held on Fridays and Saturdays since the early 19th century. This was a busy spot, especially at Christmas time when the space in front of the 'Royal Albert' was crowded with the Egg Stall's stock of Christmas trees and the local Round Table made their appeal from the base of the inn sign. BD

▼ Crown Printing Works

Now demolished. Probably one of the buildings connected to our local windmill in the first half of the 19th century, it had a boarded-up opening on the upper storey which looks as though it might have been a loft-store doorway with a hoist over it. This used to be one of the cobbled ways into the Paddock. It had been a printing firm for many years: it was founded in 1877 by Mr J A Squires. Shortly after the turn of the century a pamphlet entitled 'Picturesque Norwood' was produced by this firm combining advertisements for local traders and 'picture postcard' views of the locality. All the telephone numbers are three-figure ones on the Sydenham exchange and not a motor car in sight!.

The Printing Works were taken over by the Ward family in the 1930's. Also in this yard were the premises of F Marsh Ltd, builders, behind whose building was the Band Room used for practice by the Crystal Palace Band.

◀ **St Aubyn's Church**

The name of St Aubyn appears preserved in the wall carving dating from 1893 above the shopping parade: look over the Crystal Palace Aqua shop. The name is also used for several local roads. Curiously a Mr Orbin used to run the London Central District Industrial School (a euphemism for Workhouse for children) which occupied a large area of the Triangle, including the Church site where the School had a large array of masts and rigging upon which the boys were trained as apprentices for a career in the Merchant or the Royal Navy. These were dismantled and removed to a new site in Surrey when the site was sold for shop and housing development in the 1860s.

The church was of Kentish ragstone construction much favoured by Victorian church architects in the area. Purchased in 1864 by the London Congregational Church, it was formerly an Episcopalian Chapel. The tower was added by the Congregationalists. The church had very fine and unusual curved pews mostly lost when it was demolished.

The Croydon Churches Housing Association block of flats which now occupies the site continues the area's tradition of mild and amiable eccentricity without particularly blending with its surroundings. It won an award in Croydon's Centenary Year.
BD

▶ **St Aubyn's Road
(Off Westow Hill)**

This was graced in its heyday by a curved terrace of houses on the right hand side as you look at this picture. Bomb damage accounted for gaps in the houses and these were used as car parks. Meanwhile the remaining houses were allowed to rot away slowly until they were demolished to make way for the multi-storey part of the 'Paxton' estate. On the left-hand side houses in a similar state of disrepair have been rescued and turned into useful flats. Full marks to Hyde and South Bank Housing Association! BD

◀ 58 Gipsy Hill

A typical 1840's house. One of many treasures to be discovered by the discerning eye along the length of Gipsy Hill, which was an Enclosure road of about 1810, before that being merely a track in the Norwood Common. It has had a long association with gypsies (see other place-names: Gipsy Road (formerly Gipsy House Road), Zingari Terrace, Rommany Road, etc). Walk along Gipsy Hill and see if you can spot the former Primitive Methodist Chapel, the former Police Station, Regency cottages, and the Court Group's splendid offices on one side, and on the other, the beautifully restored terrace which had languished in decay for many years until rescued by the South London Family Housing Asosociation. Notice the English Heritage plaque! BD

▶ View down Woodland Hill, from Gipsy Hill

▼ The 'Railway Bell'

This fine inn has been 'Pub of the Year' more than once. It has a great reputation, and not only locally, as a source of 'real ale'. It has a neat beer-garden, decked with lanterns in the summer. It was built in 1892, opposite a large local dairy complete with milking parlours, the main buildings of which survive today as can be seen at the left-hand side of this picture. BD

Audrey Hammond 4.85

◄ Fox Farm and Palace Grove

Formerly the haunt of Camille Pissarro, who certainly painted both the Farm and Fox Hill, at a time when it was still probably called Fox Lane after the family who owned the farm at its foot. The farmhouse is probably the earliest building in the area. Lady Fox lived in it for many years after the death of her husband, son of one of the principal engineers involved in the design and erection of the Crystal Palace. This blissfully quiet corner is typical of the rural atmosphere so prized by the Victorians, and surely deserves to be protected from zealous tidiers of the environment as much as from rapacious developers! (See the entry in History for 1893!).

There used to be an iron bollard dated 1848 which commemorated a tour of the area by a Bishop (beating the bounds?). This and the old salt-box and the ancient gate with the 'Palace Grove' sign on it were demolished by uncaring clearers of the site with a bulldozer and no sense of history.

There used also to be lovely old lamp standards in Palace Grove. Against the wishes of the residents they were replaced by sodium lights on hideously inappropriate and ugly concrete standards. **What looks suspiciously like the originals now grace a certain housing estate in Dulwich.**
BD

"-----The roads are all
'green lanes', and in spite
of the innumerable villas, never
seem to lose their sylvan character.
The foliage, the laurels and shrubberies are
luxuriant, and the grass abounds; and with it there is a dreamy
solitude & an air of contented happiness and tranquillity...."
From 'Victoria's England' by Percy Fitzgerald 1893

Fox Hill, Upper Norwood, in 1985.

▲ Sydenham High School, 19 Westwood Hill

In the 1820's this was 'Westwood Cottage' at a time when the hill was just plain "West Hill". The building has had a varied history: at one time in its early history it was the home of Sir Sidney Colvin, the critic, who lived here with his mother.

Between 1875 and 1881 it was greatly enlarged from its smaller beginnings into something like its present size and renamed 'Horner Grange'. It was the residence of Arthur Sturt, and then of William Knight, a wealthy diamond merchant.

From 1921 to 1923 it was a Nursing Home, said astonishingly to be named 'Twilight Sleep Maternity Home', and from 1924 until 1933 it was 'Horner Grange Residential Hotel'.

It was purchased in 1933 by the GPDST to become Sydenham High School. The house had a Dining Hall complete with a minstrel's gallery and a panelled ceiling, which is still preserved as is the large stable block including a magnificent double coach-house, now the School's Craft Centre. The style is a strange melange of Gothic, Tudor and modern styles, reflecting its varied history. BD

74

◄ 86 Auckland Road

Auckland Road was developed from a 'dusty country lane' in the years between 1880 to 1885. This particular fine villa with its unusual corner gabled oriole window and attached coach-house was described at the time of its construction as a 'medium-sized villa'. It was demolished only recently, much to the regret of many local people. BD

▼ Boundary Oak, Lawrie Park Avenue

This fine oak tree stands in the centre of Lawrie Park Avenue, just by Border Road. Whoever laid out the Avenue respectfully and reverently took the road round on either side of the tree. Imagine if the Vicar's Oak still stood, as broad and noble as this one in its rightful position near the centre of the roundabout at the end of Crystal Palace Parade to mark the meeting point of Croydon, Lambeth, Bromley and Southwark! AH

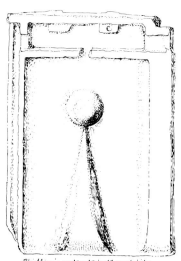

Phillips's patent lock jaw tile from 84 Auckland Road

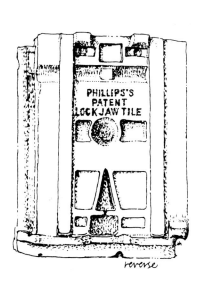

reverse

PHILLIPS'S PATENT LOCKJAW TILE

Beringer & Strohmenger

Up the dusty staircase
Past green-distempered walls
(Narrow, clattering, empty)
To the open door
Where waits the stern piano
And Miss Brownlow there.
'Have you practised this week?'
With over-glasses stare.

Brian Dann

PEOPLE: Important and interesting residents and visitors

To attempt to list all the people who have contributed to the life of the area would be an invidious task. The following is, therefore, a list including people who are either famous, interesting or important. In order not to slight the living, I have only included the very famous.

Sir William A'Beckett (1806–69)	Former Chief Justice Victoria State, Australia. Lived in Church Road 1863–69.
Mr Adams	Blacksmith, owner of forge on the present site of the 'White Swan'.
J. Corbet Anderson (1827–1907)	Author of *A History of the Parish of Croydon* and *The Great North Wood with a Geographical, Topographical and Historical Description of Upper, West & South Norwood* (1897).
T. W. Atkinson	Architect of houses adjacent to the Beulah Spa for visitors to that establishment.
Thomas Attwood (1765–1838)	Composer and musician. Pupil of Mozart and friend of Mendelssohn. Wrote Coronation Anthems for George IV and William IV. Lived at 'Roselawn', 98 Beulah Hill, 1821–34. The house has been demolished.
Earl Auckland, Lord George Eden, of Norwood (1784–1849)	Friend of William Pitt and Augustus Hervey, MP 1810–14. First Lord of the Admiralty 1834–35, Governor-General of India. Estate at Beckenham: 'Eden Park'.
Major B. S. F. Baden-Powell	Inventor and aeronaut. Re-founded Aeronautical Society 1897. Invented man-lifting kite 1894 and winged boat launched down water-chute at Crystal Palace 1902.
John Logie Baird (1888–1946)	Inventor. Television pioneer. Had laboratories at Crystal Palace (South Tower) 1933–36. Lived in Crescentwood Road, Sydenham.
Marsh Emanuel Dickinson Ball (1868–1949)	First moved to Anerley Hill after serving in the Navy to be a fireman at the Crystal Palace. In 1911 started selling papers from a barrow outside the 'White Swan'. Moved to 81 Church Road which he opened as a newsagents shop. His 16 children were all born here, including Dick Ball (qv). He opened another shop when the new row of shops was opened on the Parade.
Richard Marsh (Dick) Ball (1902–80)	Double bass player with the Ambrose Dance Orchestra from 1927 to 1941, and with many other famous bands. Trained as a musician at Greenwich Naval College fom the age of 11 – a 'grace and favour' granted to the family because of their close and continuous Naval connections: one ancestor was knighted for his contribution to the Battle of the Nile, another was an Admiral. Dick Ball bought the shop at 2 Westow Street as a retirement investment. He lived at 44 Belvedere Road until 1942 when he moved to Orleans Road.
Elsie and Jim Ballantine	In succession Membership Secretaries of the CPTCA from its inception until Elsie's death in 1985. Both of them are sadly missed.
Mr C. A. Barry	Owner of grazing land at 20 Sydenham Hill in the 1900s, one of several pasturages for the cows of French's Dairy on Gipsy Hill.
Edward Middleton Barry (1830–80)	Architect, Professor of Architecture at the Royal Academy. Designed Crystal Palace High Level Station and the 'Italian' subway linking this to the Palace. His father Charles Barry was joint architect (with Augustus Pugin) of the Palace of Westminster as well as being architect to the Alleyn Estate Governors.
William Beale	Partner in Cramer & Company, Music Publishers. Founder of the New Philharmonic Society 1855. First organised large-scale musical concerts at the Crystal Palace.
Richard Beamish	Engraver.
Joe Beesley	Proprietor of the Forge at Crown Point.

Ernest and Mrs F. A. Bellatti	Proprietors of a furniture shop whose name is preserved in the prominent brick mosaic which can still be seen on the flanking wall of their premises in Central Hill. In 1867 the Stationmaster at Gipsy Hill station was a Mr Bellatti (any relation?).
F. W. Bennett	Newsagent and inventor of the (unsuccessful) aerial bicycle (1900).
Sir William Sterndale Bennett (1816–75)	Musician and author of 'Forty Years of Music'.
Oscar Beringer (1844–1922)	Pianist. Director of the Philharmonic Society. Infant prodigy at Crystal Palace concert 1857. Continued as a regular performer there up to 1866. Beringer & Strohmenger, established in 1855, had a piano shop at the corner of Church Road and Westow Hill, behind the 'Cambridge' Public House.
Annie Besant (1847–1933)	Author, feminist, labour activist and theosophist. Lived in Colby Road off Gipsy Hill 1874. (The house bears a blue plaque.)
Sir Walter Besant (1836–1901)	Novelist and historian. Founded Society of Authors 1884 and People's Palace, Mile End Road (later East London College). *A Survey of London* (1894) and *A Survey of South London* (1912). Brother-in-law to Annie Besant.
Frank Bicknell	Owner of 'the finest billiard table manufacturers in the world', formerly in Westow Street.
Madame Helena Petrovna Blavatsky (1831–91)	Founder of the Theosophical Society in 1891. Lived at 'May Cot', Crown Dale.
Blondin (Jean François Gravelet) (1824–97)	Acrobat and tightrope walker. Walked the span of the North Transept of the Crystal Palace 1861 and also performed at several firework displays. His final appearance at the Palace was in 1871.
H. T. Bonner	Architect. Designed two houses and shops in Westow Hill 1882.
J. & C. Bowyer	Builders with a depot in Haynes Lane 1860–1961.
Charles Thomas Brock	Firework manufacturer. Initiated the famous firework displays at Crystal Palace which were known as 'Brock's Benefits'.
Robert Browning (1812–89)	Poet. Born in Camberwell, and a frequent visitor to Dulwich and the Norwood area, whose woodland walks provided him with inspiration.
Isambard Kingdom Brunel (1806–59)	Engineer. Supervised the assembly of the Crystal Palace on the Sydenham site. Designed the water towers which provided the head for the numerous elaborate fountains in the grounds.
Sir Henry Buckland (1870–1957)	General Manager, Crystal Palace Company 1920–37. Lived at 'Rockhills', Westwood Hill.
Decimus Burton (1800–81)	Architect, Fellow of the Royal Society, founder member of the Royal Institute of British Architects. Designed and landscaped Beulah Spa, including the pump and assembly rooms and Tivoli Lodge, which still stands at the entrance to the former spa on Spa Hill off Beulah Hill. The lower portion of Grange Road was previously called Decimus Burton Road after him.
Frank Hedges Butler (1855–1928)	Wine merchant and amateur balloonist. Founder of the (Royal) Aero Club 1901. (The 'Royal' was added in 1910.)
Admiral John Byng (1704–1757)	Friend of Augustus Hervey (qv), who served under him before becoming Earl of Bristol, and was a loyal friend to him even when he was court-martialled and shot 'to encourage the others'. He left Hervey a splendid French clock which remained at 'Norwood House' until the death of Mary Nesbitt.
Frederick Bywaters (1902–23)	Murderer. One of the defendants in the notorious Thompson-Bywaters murder case, he was apprehended at his mother's house 11 Westow Street, since demolished to provide access to the Paxton estate.

Sir Francis Campbell (1832–1914)	Founder and Principal of the Royal Normal College for the Blind. Lived at 'Windermere', Church Road. His son Guy succeeded him as Principal from 1912–1929.
Thomas Campbell (1777–1844)	Poet, critic, journalist and editor of *Specimens of British Poetry*. Lived in Sydenham 1804–42. Author of many school recitation pieces as well as a biography of Mrs Sarah Siddons, the well-known actress. He is buried in Westminster Abbey.
Mr Carber(r)y	Butcher, of Westow Street. A picture dated 1870 shows him in top hat standing proudly before his carcase-decorated shopfront on the corner of what is now Carberry Road. The name of the shop is shown as 'Carbery', which may be the error of the engraver. He was an ancestor of the Snelling family who run the Crystal Palace Camping shop.
Harry Cardwell (1912–79)	A founder and organiser of the Upper Norwood Association for Community Care (UNACC) 1973.
Plantagenet Pierrepoint Carey, 11th Viscount Falkland (1806–86)	Admiral of the Fleet. Lived at 'Falkland Park', a large mansion on Beggar's Hill (South Norwood Hill) now part of the premises of Spurgeon's College. Buried in All Saints' Churchyard.
William Carruthers (1830–1922)	Keeper of the Botanical Department, British Museum of Natural History.
Samuel Franklin Cody	American inventor, became a naturalised Englishman. He invented man-lifting kites (1905) and the first dirigible airship (1907).
Samuel Coleridge-Taylor (1875–1912)	Composer, of *Hiawatha* fame. Conducted performances at Crystal Palace. Born in South Norwood and lived for many years in Norbury.
Sir Ninian Comper (1864–1960)	Church Architect and stained glass artist. His work is incorporated into St John's Church in Auckland Road. First President of the Norwood Society. Lived at 'The Priory', Beulah Hill 1912–1960.
Jack Compton (1882–1958)	Rolls-Royce and Bentley specialist. Had premises in Westow Street 1934–1958.
Ronnie Corbett (1930–)	Comedian and TV personality. Lived in Church Road during the late 1960s, moving from the area in 1971.
Sir Michael Costa (1810–84)	Composer and conductor of the Crystal Palace Band. Founder of Concert Pitch. Organised the first Handel Festival at Crystal Palace 1857. Conducted Handel Festivals every year until 1877.
Mr Coulson	Proprietor of the Anerley Tea Gardens 1841–1868.
David Cox (junior) (1809–85)	Watercolourist. Lectured at Crystal Palace School of Art. Buried in West Norwood Cemetery.
John Crawley	Hotelier and publican, owner of the Park Hotel on Central Hill 1837–47.
Lionel Crossley	Speedway rider and author of a book *Crystal Palace Speedway*, published by the Crystal Palace Foundation, which recalls the track opened in 1928 at the Crystal Palace.
Charles Robert Darwin (1809–82)	Naturalist and friend among others of Fitzroy (qv). He was an occasional visitor to Church Road and to the Palace, where he made the acquaintance of Arthur Sullivan (qv).
H. Day	Furniture remover and warehouseman at 240 Gipsy Road in the 1900s. A contemporary advertisement shows the typical broad, open-topped horse-drawn pantechnicon of the turn of the century.
Miss Elizabeth Louisa Dee	Local historian, author of *Memories of Norwood since 1852*. She lived in Oxford Road.
Captain, Sir Geoffrey De Havilland (1882–1965)	Famous aircraft designer. Started his career by training at the Crystal Palace School of Engineering from 1900 to 1903.

Walter De La Mare (1873–1956)	Poet and author. Lived in Waldegrave Road before he moved to Twickenham.
Philip Henry Delamotte (1820–89)	Photographer. Produced complete photographic record of the construction of the Crystal Palace at Sydenham which was published in 1855.
Thomas Dermody (1775–1802)	Poet. Lived at Sydenham during the last years of his life.
Edward Rimbault Dibdin (1883–1941)	Littérateur, artist and critic. Lived in South Croxted Road.
William Joseph Dibdin (1850–1925)	Chemist. Lived in Idmiston Road.
Charles Dickens (1812–70)	Journalist and novelist. A frequent visitor to 'Springfield', a splendid house formerly 105 Beulah Hill, opposite Queen Mary's Road. It is said that he wrote much of *David Copperfield* sitting under the shade of the still surviving cedar tree in the grounds. The house and garden are the scene of several incidents in *David Copperfield*. The church David and Dora visited in that novel must have been All Saints'. Dickens also visited the Crystal Palace and had many friends in Dulwich.
Frank Dickson (1862–1936)	Landscape painter. Lived at 'Parkside', Farquhar Road.
Eugene Arnold Dolmetsch (1858–1940)	Musician, musicologist and pioneer in the revival of both early music and instruments. Taught at Dulwich College 1885–95. Lived successively at 4 Alleyn Crescent, 60 Croxted Road and 'Dowland', 172 Rosendale Road, which he found the perfect setting for 'Home Music' as his friends and supporters, George Grove and Bernard Shaw among them, would agree. His famous collection of early musical instruments is now in the Ranger's House, Greenwich, under the care of the staff of the Horniman Museum.
Henrietta le Forestier D'Osseville	Founder of Virgo Fidelis Convent, in Central Hill, 1847.
Sir Arthur Conan Doyle (1859–1930)	Author and spiritualist. Lived in South Norwood. It is said that he used 'Little Menlo' as the model for 'Pondicherry Lodge' in *The Sign of Four*. *The Norwood Builder* is probably set in Church Road. He lived in Tennison Road, South Norwood. The house bears a blue plaque.
Mr Dubbens	Bookshop proprietor in Westow Street from 1862.
Lawrence Durrell (1912–)	Author of the *Black Book* which is set in and shows a great familiarity with the Crystal Palace area.
Sextus Dyball	Architect; designed the extension and new building for the 'White Hart' in 1868 and a number of Tyrolean-style houses in Church Road including the splendidly gothic No 128, a listed building.
John M. East (1860–1924)	Producer and Impresario. Organised dramatic martial firework displays on the Crystal Palace football ground 1909. Made Royal Navy recruiting film at Crystal Palace 1915.
Sir Edward Elgar (1857–1934)	Composer of chamber, symphonic, choral and brass band music. Stayed for about a year at 'Oaklands', College Road 1889–1890. Several visits later in connection with musical events at Crystal Palace, including Brass Band festivals for which he wrote many competition pieces.
C. E. Englebach	Owner of 'Holderness House' in the 1900s. The extensive grazing this provided was used for grazing by French's cows. Before Mr Englebach or his predecessor Mr Maudslay (qv) had lived here, the site was occupied for hundreds of years by a windmill.
James Epps	Cocoa and chocolate manufacturer. Lived at 'Bigginwood House', Biggin Hill. Buried at West Norwood cemetery. In his day Epps was a household name; the motto of his cocoa: 'Grateful and Comforting'.
Dr John Epps (1805–69)	Homeopathic doctor, Director of the Royal Jennerian and London Vaccine Institute. Friend of politicians Giuseppe

	Mazzini and Lajos Kossuth. Lived at 'White Lodge' on Biggin Hill.
4th Earl and Countess of Essex	She a singer (Kitty Spencer) at the Beulah Spa, he an octogenarian. They lived at 'Essex Court' on Central Hill. Read all about them in Joan Warwick's interesting booklet on the history of the Beulah Spa, obtainable from the Norwood Society.
Richard Cadman Etches (–1817)	Royal Naval Intelligence agent. Active in France during the time of the French Revolution. Lived on Beulah Hill.
J. Etherington	Tailor, at 26 Church Road in the 1900s.
John Evelyn (1620–1706)	Diarist. Visited the area several times. In 1675 he was attacked and robbed near the Vicar's Oak. As well as his diaries he also wrote *Fumufugium*, a treatise on London's air pollution.
A. J. Eyre	Organist from 1889–93 at the Crystal Palace, and also at St John's Church 'while it was still an Iron Church'.
Thomas Farquhar	Solicitor and Secretary of the Crystal Palace Company, after whom Farquhar Road is named.
Mr Ferrier	Grocer in 1867, on the corner of Gipsy Hill and George Street (later renamed Cawnpore Street).
Elaine Fifield (1930–)	Ballerina, formerly with Sadlers Wells Opera Ballet, subsequently the Royal Ballet, until 1958. Later Ballerina with the Australian Ballet, until 1969. Her autobiography *In My Shoes* was published in 1967. Born in Australia she lived in South Norwood while dancing in this country.
Bridget Finch (–1768)	Queen of the Gypsies 1740–68, in succession to her aunt, Margaret. Buried in Dulwich Burial Ground.
Elizabeth Finch	Granddaughter of Margaret who succeeded Bridget in 1768!
Margaret Finch (1636–1740)	Queen of the Norwood Gypsies. Lived by the 'Gypsy House' which stood near to where

	Gipsy Hill Station is now. She had 16 children, all named after flowers! Due to her habit of sitting resting her chin on her knees, she had to be buried in a large square coffin. Buried at Beckenham.
Vice-Admiral Robert Fitzroy (1805–65)	Hydrographer, meteorologist, former commander HMS *Beagle*, and governor, until 1845, of New Zealand. Lived at 'Lyndhurst', 140 Church Road (since demolished).
Edward Fletcher	Proprietor of a Glove and Haberdashery shop, located in premises over the South Door of the Palace in the 1900s.
Elsie Fogerty (1865–1945)	Founder of the Central School of Speech Training and Dramatic Art. Formerly lecturer in English and Speech at the Crystal Palace School of Art 1889–1912.
Amédée Forestier (–1930)	Black and white graphic artist, worked for *Illustrated London News*.
Sir Charles Fox (1810–74)	Engineer and founder of the firm of Fox, Henderson and Partners who drew up the detailed designs for the Crystal Palace and oversaw its construction both at Hyde Park and at Sydenham, a service for which he was knighted. His son Sir Francis Fox was also famous for his restoration work.
Mr Franklin	Cobbler in Westow Street. Listed in directory of 1853.
Emperor Frederick III (of Germany) (1831–88)	Stayed at the 'Queen's Hotel' to breathe the Norwood air ('the finest anywhere') for his health in 1887.
J. H. Fricker	Stationer and Bookseller of 84 Westow Hill and 8 Church Road in the 1900s. He also sold Venetian glass and 'white wood for poker work'.
A. Galer	Local historian. Author of *Norwood and Dulwich, Past and Present* (1890).
Bertram Gallannaugh	Architect. Designed Franklin Roosevelt Memorial, Grosvenor Square. Lived in Fountain Drive.

Dr E. W. Gandy (1879–1958)	General Practitioner and Police Surgeon. Lived at 'Hill Top' at the top of Gipsy Hill.
Rev. D. W. Garrow	Local historian. Author of *The History and Antiquities of Croydon* (1818).
King George III (1738–1820)	Visited the Norwood Gypsies when Prince of Wales. Visited Mary Nesbitt's house to attend meetings of the Privy Council.
King George IV (1762–1830)	Visited Beulah Spa and Sydenham Wells.
Mrs Gilbert	Local historian. Author of memoir: *All Saints' Church, Upper Norwood and the parish which it served during the 19th century.*
John Giles	Architect of Christ Church, Gipsy Hill 1867, and the tower, vestry and Parish Hall added in 1889.
James Glaisher (1809–1903)	Superintendent of the Magnetical and Meteorological section of the Royal Observatory, Greenwich, 1861 onwards. Ascended to 24,163 feet in balloon from the Crystal Palace grounds 1863. Lived at 'The Shola', Croydon.
Frederick William Goodliffe (1875–1947)	Lived in Whiteley Road, then at 3 Gipsy Hill, finally moving to Beulah Hill in 1920. In 1900 he started the New Century Window Cleaning Company, based in Holborn where his large family of descendants and relatives continue to run the family cleaning business, now greatly enlarged to form the OCS Group. He and his wife (née Westwood) had 3 sons and 5 daughters. The family have continued to live in the area and have been generous benefactors throughout their association with it, particularly to Christ Church which owed its piano, and a stained glass window to them, as well as the funds for the new church hall, named the 'Goodliffe Hall' to commemorate the fact.
Dr William G. Grace (1848–1915)	Cricketer, player-manager of the London County Cricket Club based at the Crystal Palace.
	Lived at Lawrie Park Road 1889–1909.
Claude Grahame-White (1879–1959)	Aeronautical pioneer. First flew at Crystal Palace 1910. Associate of the Aerial Manufacturing Company based at Crystal Palace.
Sir George Grove (1820–1900)	Engineer, archaeologist, musicologist and musician. Secretary and Director of the Crystal Palace Company from 1852 to 1882. Pioneer musicologist and author and editor of the famous *Grove's Dictionary of Music*. First Director of the Royal College of Music 1882 to 1894. Lived at 'Grove House', Church Meadow, Lower Sydenham.
Sir H. Rider Haggard (1856–1925)	Novelist and explorer. Settled in Norwood 1881–1882. Is it a mere coincidence that one of the founders of the Upper Norwood Athenaeum society was a Henry Goodall Quartermain? Readers of *King Solomon's Mines* will note the similarity to the names of two of Rider Haggard's heroes!
Miss Sarah Jane Halifax	Principal, in 1867, of 'Orford College' which stood on the station side of Gipsy Hill, just below the present Gipsy Hill Hotel.
Henry Hall (1898–)	Famous leader of the BBC Dance Orchestra in the 1930s. Lived in Grange Road.
Rev. Edmund Harden (1796–1856)	Curate in charge All Saints' Chapel 1829–45. Vicar of All Saints' Church 1845–56 and buried in its churchyard. See Audrey Hammond's personal recollections in this book.
Rolf Harris (1930–)	Australian-born comedian, artist and TV personality. Lived for several years in Border Road, Sydenham.
B. Waterhouse Hawkins	Sculptor, and later Director of the Fossil Department at the Crystal Palace. Hawkins sculpted the famous reconstructions of prehistoric animals in the Park.
Walter Hedgecock (1864–1932)	Organist, conductor and composer, among other works,

	of the musical setting of Rudyard Kipling's *On the Road to Mandalay*. Was organist at All Saints' Church for a number of years, as well as performing and conducting at the Crystal Palace.
John Hennessey (1829–1910)	Deputy Surveyor-General of India. Lived on retirement in Alleyn Park.
King Henry I (reigned 1100–35)	Had a hunting lodge 'in Dulwich Vale' on present site of 'Kingswood House'.
Augustus Hervey, 3rd Earl of Bristol (1724–79)	Served under Admiral Byng (qv) until coming into the title; lived with Mary Nesbitt on Central Hill in 'Norwood House', a much enlarged cottage which has now become Virgo Fidelis convent school.
Dr Frederick Hetley	Owned 'Norbury Lodge', 'Highland Lodge' and 'Rose Cottage' at one time.
Henry Heynes (1849–1925)	Builder and undertaker, lived at 44 Westow Street, and opened a hardware shop there. Haynes Lane where he built 6 houses for his 6 daughters is named after him, but the council never corrected their spelling mistake! He was succeeded by his son, who lived at 52 Gipsy Hill. Miss Heynes, his granddaughter, was born in and still lives in the family home in Gipsy Hill. The original shop was eventually taken over as a solicitor's office.
George Highton	Architect. Designed 'Grecian Villa', Beulah Hill, now St Joseph's College.
Rev. Walter Hobbs (1843–1914)	Pastor of the Gipsy Road Baptist Chapel for 35 years. Guardian of the Poor. Chaplain to West Norwood Cemetery.
Alfred Hollins (1865–1942)	Organist and composer and former pupil at the Royal Normal College. He was official organist at Crystal Palace and was also the organist at St Andrew's Presbyterian Church 1888–97. He was also organist at the People's Palace, Mile End Road, so he seems to have been busy, yet he found time to write a book *A Blind Musician Looks Back* (1936).
Leslie Howard (1893–1943)	Stage and film actor. His mother, Lilian Stainer, founded the Upper Norwood Dramatic Club 1912. Lived as a boy at 'Allandale', Jasper Road, and later on Sydenham Hill.
J. Jewhurst	Architect. Designed and supervised the rebuilding of the 'White Swan' in 1885, replacing the smaller building with its adjacent extensive Tea Gardens and stabling which had graced the site before.
Mr & Mrs Jinks	Proprietors of the Windmill Tea Gardens which lay at the bend of Paddock Passage, adjacent to the Windmill which was pulled down shortly after the tea gardens opened in 1853!
John Lawson Johnston (1839–1900)	Pioneer dietician: 'Mr Bovril', the founder of the company of that name. Lived at 'Kingswood', Sydenham Hill, and was buried in West Norwood Cemetery.
George Albert Jones (1881–1955)	Manager of Crystal Palace General Iron Foundry (1912–34).
Owen Jones (1809–74)	Artist and decorator. Joint Director of Decoration at the Crystal Palace from 1852 onwards.
Reuben Kelf-Cohen (1899–1981)	Founder of the Norwood Society.
Caton N. Laid	Designer of ironwork screens.
Samuel Laing MP (1812–1907)	Chairman of the Crystal Palace Company from 1852 onwards. Chairman of the London, Brighton and Southern Railway 1867–1894. Lived at 'Rockhills' after the death of Paxton. Wrote many books expounding Darwinism in popular form when in his 70s.
Lillie Langtry (1853–1929)	Actress and intimate friend of Edward VII. Lived at 'Whitehall' on South Norwood Hill. The building fell into decrepitude and was demolished to make way for a block of flats.
Dr Leese	Held pastures in Upper and Lower Norwood, 1820 onwards. Lived in Central Hill.

H. Letheren	Manufacturing confectioner at 20 Gipsy Hill in the 1900s.
Franz Liszt (1811–86)	Composer and virtuoso pianist. Conducted concerts at the Crystal Palace. Stayed at 'Westwood House', Westwood Hill.
Margaret Lockwood (1916–)	Stage and film actress. Lived Lunham Road 1916–19 then moved to Highland Road. She attended Sydenham High School as a pupil.
Owen Luder (1928–)	President (1975–78) and Honorary Architect of Norwood Society. Past president RIBA. Lived for a time at 'Innisfail', Beulah Hill.
Sir August Manns (1825–1907)	Conductor and Musical Director of the Crystal Palace Band, later expanded to form a full orchestra. He introduced the music of Brahms, Schubert and Schumann to audiences at the Crystal Palace. Directed the Handel festivals from 1883 to 1900. Lived in Harold Road and later at 'White Lodge', Biggin Hill, where he died. He was buried at West Norwood Cemetery.
Catherine Marsh (1818–1912)	Welfare worker for the 'navvies' who built the Crystal Palace. Organised soup kitchens for them and their dependants 1854. Peacemaker at the 'Battle of Penge' between rival gangs of navvies in 1854. Recruited navvies for pioneer works in the Crimea.
James Martin	Cowkeeper, of Westow Street, 1823 to 1866.
Gerald Massey (1828–1907)	Poet and mystic, Christian socialist. Lived at 'Redcot', South Norwood Hill.
Thomas Henry Maudslay	Son of the founder of a famous engineering firm, he was the owner of 'Holderness House' at Crown Point. The house itself stood where Furneaux Avenue is now. The Holderness Estate covers much of the former gardens and grounds; Knight's Hill Recreation Ground was created in 1914 from the remainder.
Sir Hiram Maxim (1840–1916)	American-born inventor of the machine gun, and of the sensational Maxim's Flying Machine at the Crystal Palace. Buried at West Norwood.
Felix Mendelssohn (1809–47)	Composer. Visited Upper Norwood where he stayed with his friend Thomas Attwood (qv). Some of his works are noted as having been 'written at Norwood'.
Stanley Edward Morrison (1908–85)	Harpist. Born in Rommany Road, West Norwood, he started his working life as a Cullens' Funeral Director, but always had the ambition to play the harp. He trained under Lucy Phelps and eventually became a professional harpist at the age of 35, with the BBC Northern Symphony Orchestra, then the Bournemouth Symphony Orchestra and finally with the Sadlers Wells Orchestra. From 1961 he lived in Wharncliffe Gardens, off South Norwood Hill.
Thomas Moy	Aeronautical pioneer, inventor of several steam-driven flying machines exhibited at the Crystal Palace. His 'Aerial Steamer' was a heroic failure in 1871.
John Muirhead (1863–1927)	Artist and illustrator. Lived on Gipsy Hill.
Edward Nash	Architect. Designed enlargement and additions to All Saints' Church.
Joseph Nash	'Specialist in the Foot and its Covering' – a sort of combined chiropodist and bootmaker. Established 1881; he had consultation rooms in Westow Street at least until the 1900s.
Mary Nesbitt (1745–1835)	Widow of Mr Nesbitt, banker and a member of the de Crespigny family of Camberwell, became the mistress of Augustus Hervey (qv); lived in 'Norwood House' a converted and enlarged cottage on Central Hill which later became first the 'Park Hotel' and subsequently the Junior School part of Virgo Fidelis convent school. She was

	a close associate of members of the government of William Pitt, and Privy Council meetings were held at her home during the reign of King George III. She was alleged to have acted as a secret government agent abroad.
Sir Joseph Paxton (1801–65)	Landscape gardener and architect of the Crystal Palace. He also designed the gardens of 'The Wood' and the Dulwich Wood House public house on Sydenham Hill. Lived at 'Rockhills' on Westwood Hill. Only the gateposts remain.
W. T. Phillips	Local historian. Author of *Norwood in Days of Old* (1912).
Camille Pissarro (1830–1903)	Impressionist painter. Lived, married and painted in Crystal Palace area 1871–72. Several of his paintings depict local scenes, including Fox Hill, Crystal Palace Parade and All Saints' Church. Lived at 2 Chatham Terrace, Palace Road (now demolished), and at 77a Westow Hill (see the blue plaque provided by the Crystal Palace Foundation and the National Westminster Bank).
'Pa' Poirin (–1933)	From 1910 onwards until his death, 'Pa' organised sports and gymnastics for the young people of the Christ Church congregation.
F. Pouget	Architect. Designed extension to the 'Queen's Hotel' 1887, and 'Norbury Lodge' at the corner of Fox Hill and Church Road.
J. Pringle	Ironmonger, gas and hot water fitter of 61–63 Westow Street in the 1900s.
Sir Vincent Sawdon (V. S.) Pritchett (1900–)	Novelist, short story writer and critic. Educated at Alleyn's School. Lived as a boy at 200 Clive Road and knew the Upper Norwood area and the Crystal Palace well.
Ebenezer Prout (1853–1909)	Musician, musicologist. Assistant Professor at Crystal Palace School of Art 1868–84.
W. Purcell	Owner of 'Beaulieu', South Norwood Hill, in the 1900s, now a home for mentally handicapped people, and whose grounds accommodate the communications station of the IBA with its aerial tower, as well as providing a woodland walk down to Auckland Road.
'Miss Read' (Mrs Dora Saint) (1913–)	Novelist. Lived in Upper Norwood.
Sims Reeves (1818–1900)	Singer. Lived at 'Grange Mount' at corner of Grange Road and Beulah Hill.
John Rennie (1761–1821)	Civil Engineer. Builder of the Croydon Canal which ran through South Norwood, past the 'Jolly Sailor' tea-gardens, to Anerley (the Anerley Tea-Gardens) and up to the Grand Union Canal. South Norwood lake was originally a reservoir for this canal. The canal opened in 1809 and closed 1836.
Jean Rhys (1894–1979)	Novelist. Lived at 2a Milestone Road 1952–53.
John Ruskin (1819–1900)	Critic and writer. He knew the Norwood Hills from his time in Camberwell: 'the Norwood hills, partly rough with furze, partly wooded with birch and oak, partly in pure green bramble copse and rather steep pasture which rose with the promise of all the rustic loveliness of Surrey and Kent in them . . .'
John Scott Russell (1808–82)	Civil engineer, member of the original Exhibition Committee which commissioned the Crystal Palace in 1851, and adviser to the Crystal Palace Company. Refused Arthur Sullivan his daughter's hand in marriage. Sullivan was to remain a bachelor all his life. Russell lived near Crystal Palace.
Ken Russell (1927–)	Film and TV director. His first film had the Crystal Palace High Level Station as its location. Lived for a time at 124 Church Road. He is remembered locally for his habit of barefoot walking and for insisting that Bradley's stock Palladio wallpapers, in the days when it was a general builder's merchants!
James Savage (1779–1852)	Architect. Designed the original All Saints' Church 1827–29.

A. A. Saward	Local historian. Author of *Reminiscences of Norwood*: published by Upper Norwood Literary and Scientific Society, 1907.
Leo Schuster	Landowner of Penge Park, who sold the site to the Crystal Palace Company in 1853 for £50,000. He was also a Director of the London, Brighton and South Coast Railway.
Thomas Scott (1808–78)	Explorer, hunter and freethinker. Page at the court of Charles X (of France). Lived in Norwood 1870–78.
John Shaw (1776–1832)	Architect. Designed 'Beaulieu Heights' at the top of South Norwood Hill.
James Lumsden Skene (1879–1955)	Journalist. Reporter on the *Norwood News*. Became Advertising Manager of *Streatham News*.
John Davidson Smith	Owner and developer of the Beulah Spa.
Samuel Leigh Sotheby (1771–1842)	Auctioneer and antiquary; nephew of the founder of the famous firm. Lived at 'Woodlands', Beulah Hill, later replaced by the present blocks of flats.
Stanley Spencer	Balloonist and aeronaut. The first Englishman to fly a powered balloon, which he did at Crystal Palace in 1902.
Charles Haddon Spurgeon (1834–92)	Baptist preacher and evangelist. Preached to 23,654 people at Crystal Palace, 1857. His funeral at West Norwood was an occasion for national mourning. Lived at 'Westwood', a large house off Beulah Hill. Spurgeon Road follows the line of the former drive.
Oliver Stallybrass (1925–78)	Editor, translator, former Assistant Librarian, the London Library. Co-Editor *The Dictionary of Modern Thought*; Editor, Abinger Edition of the works of E. M. Forster. Translated many Scandinavian writers into English. Lived on Westwood Hill.
A. J. Steele	Watchmaker, jeweller and optician of 24 Westow Street about 1900.
F. Stevens	'The People's Stationer' of 50 Westow Street – publisher of a Local View Book 'entirely free from advertisements' and costing 6½d in the 1900s.
T. W. Stoughton (1884–1917)	Publisher (founded the firm of Hodder and Stoughton in 1868), evangelist and philanthropist. Founded Auckland Hill Evangelical Church. Lived in Gipsy Road and at 32 Beulah Hill. Buried in West Norwood Cemetery.
Johann Strauss (1825–99)	Viennese composer and bandmaster. Frequently attended and conducted at Beulah Spa.
Sir Arthur Sullivan (1842–1900)	Composer and Professor of Musical Composition and Ballad Singing at the Crystal Palace School of Art. The first performance of his 'Tempest' was given at Crystal Palace in 1862, and was attended among others by Charles Darwin who congratulated the young composer on his achievement. Sullivan went on to fame and fortune as the composer, with W. S. Gilbert, of the popular D'Oyly Carte comic operas. Sullivan's death was caused by a fall between the platform and the footboard of a train at Sydenham Hill station.
Spike Sullivan	Boxer and former employee at the 'Albany' cinema in Church Road.
Basil Sydney (1894–1968)	Stage and film actor. Lived locally.
Walter Taylor	Nurseryman, seedsman and florist, of The Nursery, Church Road, in the 1900s. The large greenhouses extended down the slopes to the edge of the Cintra Estate.
Lord Edward Thurlow (1731–1806)	Eminent lawyer. Solicitor General 1770, Attorney General 1771, Lord Chancellor 1778–1792. Owner of extensive estates locally, starting with Knight's Hill Farm at Tulse Hill, bought to accommodate his

	mistress Polly Humphreys. Later he acquired other land stretching from Herne Hill to Lower Norwood, forming the enormous Thurlow Estate, which proved so difficult to dispose of as a single plot of land after his death.
Sir Charles Ernest Tritton MP (1845–1918)	MP for Norwood. Proprietor of Brightwen & Co. Director of the UK Provident Institute. Contributed towards the cost of making Norwood Park public. Author of *An Illustrated Account of Norwood, Forest Hill, Dulwich and district* (1893). Lived at 'Bloomfield Hall', Central Hill.
Martin Farquhar Tupper (1810–89)	Poet and unsuccessful inventor. Lived at 'Underhill', 13 Cintra Park, 1880–1889.
Mme Marie Tussaud (1760–1850)	Originator of the famous Waxworks museum. Befriended by Mary Nesbitt, she is said to have lived at 'Effingham Lodge', 69 Central Hill.
Lord Vestey (1866–1940)	Shipping magnate ('Blue Star Line') and director of the Union Cold Storage Company, among numerous others. He lived at 'Kingswood', now the Community Centre and Library at the heart of the Kingswood estate. Lord Vestey had his own private entrance to Sydenham Hill station!
T. C. Walters (–1955)	Founder and Director of Crystal Palace Football Club. The club used to be based on the Crystal Palace site. He was the proprietor of a high-class provision store at 66 Westow Hill.
Jesse Ward	Founder of the *Croydon Advertiser*, printer of the first edition of 'Norwood News' 1868.
J. Randall Waring	Architect. Designed new stable block for the 'Queen's Hotel' 1885.
Mr Warren	Butcher. Listed as trading in Westow Street 1853 Directory.
Alan R. Warwick (1900–73)	Local historian. Chairman Norwood Society 1961–1970. Vice President 1970–73 Author

	of *The Phoenix Suburb*. His was the third generation of his family to have lived at 'The Sycamores' 75 Beulah Hill.
Professor F. E. Weiss (1865–1953)	Assistant Professor of Botany, University College, London. Lived at Norbury Lodge Hotel, Fox Hill.
Miss Elsa West (1884–1971)	Lived with her sister at 'Pen-Y-Bryn' on the corner of Fox Hill and Tudor Road, the house which appears in Pissarro's painting of Fox Hill. She was a notable pianist and musician, founder of 'Norwood Music' and organised an annual local St Cecilia's Festival.
Mr and Mrs Wickenden	He was a carter, she the proprietor of a beer shop in 1867. By 1869 this had become the 'Railway Bell' of which Harriet Wickenden became the first hostess. By that time there were seven private houses in Cawnpore Street as well as a row of cottages for letting, 'Malta Cottages'.
Kaiser Wilhelm II (of Germany) (1859–1941)	Stayed at the 'Queen's Hotel' on several occasions between 1900 and 1906.
James Benson Wilson (1905–49)	West Norwood undertaker and local historian. He was the 5th James Benson Wilson, the first having been born in 1830!
Joseph William Wilson	Engineer. First Principal of the Crystal Palace School of Practical Engineering. His son was President of the same institution.
W. E. Wiltshire	Owner of the Avenue Meadow off Gipsy Hill in the 1900s, where French's dairy cattle could be seen grazing.
Mrs Henry Wood (1814–87)	Author of many popular novels. Lived in Gipsy Hill from 1856, in Palace Road in 1860 and stayed subsequently at Belvedere Road. Perhaps her most famous work is *East Lynne*, written at Upper Norwood.
Robin Wood	Founder of the Robin Wood 'Emancipation' Garage 1896. Pioneer in the use of wind power to provide electricity.

William Frederick Woodington (1806–93)	Sculptor. He made the large bust of Joseph Paxton which is still in the Crystal Palace Sports Centre. This was originally installed in the Palace grounds in 1873 to commemorate 20 years of the Palace, and in honour of its originator.	**Sir Mathew Digby Wyatt (1820–77)**	Architect and art critic. Secretary to the Executive Committee for the Great Exhibition of 1851. Designed courts for the Sydenham Crystal Palace with Owen Jones.
Mr Wright	Carter, living in one of the only two houses in College Street off Gipsy Hill in 1867. (By 1869 there were nine houses.) This road still exists, but now forms the bottom part of Woodland Road.	**Emile Zola (1840–1902)**	Stayed in Upper Norwood (at the 'Queen's Hotel') in 1894 and while a refugee during the Dreyfus scandal which he had publicised by his famous article 'J'Accuse'.

The entrance to Rockhills, home of Sir Joseph Paxton, now the northern gateway to the Crystal Palace Park

My Last Crystal Palace Circus 1936

All the way from Tottenham
By bus we rode for treats
And come to the Crystal Palace
Clutching our bags of sweets.

We've come to see the Circus
We've come to see the clowns
We've come to see the lady
In her spangled riding gown.

I don't like acrobats,
And I don't like to see
Animals made fools of
By human cruelty.

The people sit in circles
About the Circus ring
But we sit in the choir 'Gods'
So we see everything.

I like the organ pipes so tall
The polished wood and brass.
I love this dusty Palace
And its walls all made of glass.

I'm so glad we're moving
To be near this place
I love the funny 'Courts'
I love the sense of space.

I love the Crystal Fountain
And the statues and the Maze
I love the great big gardens
And I love Brock's Benefit days.

I'm so looking forward
To coming here to stay!
A wonder like this Palace
Will never go away!   **Brian Dann**

WHERE DO WE GO FROM HERE?

Well, there it is: our rather superficial look at Crystal Palace/Norwood Heights, call it what you will, it's *our* place. The history we have given is spotty; we know there are gaps, there may well be inaccuracies, though we have done our best in the time and with the limited resources available, to remove these. There is certainly room for a more careful, considered and accurate examination of the evidence than we have provided here. Certainly we could well have produced an equally interesting, though much larger book detailing much more of the people and places of the area; so many families seem to have stayed in the area for many generations, even today.

Is there any further Treasure Trove to be discovered where once the Great North Wood spread the noble branches of its oaks? What can be gleaned from local and Romany folklore and oral history? Are there any other traces of 'unwritten history'? Fossils? Archeological remains? Does the stump of the Westow Hill windmill still exist in debris somewhere in the remaining unbuilt portions of the Paddock, now fenced off?

We have barely touched the large corpus of written and printed material, maps and pictures to be found about this area to be found in the Library Collections of Bromley, Croydon, Lambeth, Lewisham and Southwark. We are most grateful for the help given to us by the staff of Upper Norwood Library, and in particular, Pat Scott and Jerry Savage and to the other people mentioned in our list of acknowledgements. Our facts have

Capital in Church Road

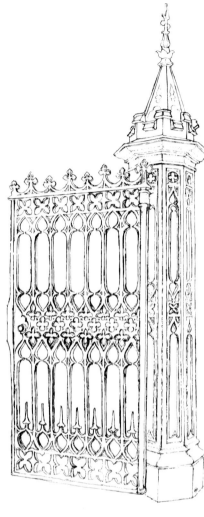

Decorative cast iron gate and gate post of All Saints Church yard

been drawn mainly from the Local History collection of Upper Norwood Library. But there is more, much more to be discovered. Perhaps one day someone will attempt this fuller and more daunting task. Whoever does this will need the dynamic help of someone like Robin Redsull, a gifted and energetic organiser without whose efforts this book would have continued to lanquish unpublished while the loss of character of the Crystal Palace area continued unchecked!

It is interesting to compare the fates, in retrospect, of Dulwich, a village in a valley, and Crystal Palace, a village on a hill. For Dulwich has been blessed for the several centuries since Edward Alleyn's bequest with a single governing authority which has ensured that with few exceptions it has preserved its character. In contrast, although Crystal Palace has been blessed with the large parkland of the Palace site, which has prevented it from sinking unmarked into the unhindered developments of other London suburbs, it has been subject to the largely uncoordinated planning efforts of five London Boroughs. Each of these planning authorities has tended to view the problems of the area as peripheral to its central concerns, and in the main to make decisions which took little or no regard of what lay immediately across their own border. With several local amenity groups acting sometimes in equally uncoordinated ways Crystal Palace's unique character has not been served as well as it might.

A more hopeful and positive aspect of the area is the continuing presence of people and businesses with unique skills.

In its heyday there were two piano and music shops, of which the last to survive is featured on the front cover. Several dress shops and gentlemen's outfitters, a billiard-table maker, a doll manufacturer and several printing firms had

profitable businesses at one time. Many of these depended for their success on the proximity of the Palace or a wealthy clientele. At one time we had no fewer than three cinemas: the 'Electric' (now a Billiard and Snooker Hall but between times a swimming baths, a printers and 'Jacatex's' clothing stores), the 'Albany' and the 'Rialto' in Church Road, one now a car showroom, the other a Bingo club.

In later years furniture restoration has been a staple industry, and we still have a gilder and a stone worker. We have the new enterprise of 'Alley Arts', the home of the Gipsy Hill Craft Co-op, offering the first glimmering of rekindled hope in what once seemed a lost cause: the CPTCA idea of a family Arts Centre within the Triangle. And now we have UNIT with some parliamentary clout and the plans of the London Borough of Bromley to restore some of the prestige and business to the area. Bromley's detailed plans to restore the quality of the Crystal Palace site by landscaping improvements are already visible in the park furniture and the beautiful restoration of the once-crumbling terraces. There are proposals for a hotel on the Palace site.

The London Borough of Croydon have recently introduced some marginal environmental improvements around the Triangle. It is fervently to be hoped that this represents a genuine re-think of Croydon's past attitudes. Otherwise this investment of a few thousands will prove an ineffective gesture from a borough which elsewhere is prepared to invest £11 million in a super new swimming pool!

There is a lot of past to live down: look for instance at the poor quality of the detailing and specification of the public portions of the Norwood Heights development. Did *you* realise that the grass area along the Safeway frontage belongs to Croydon Council? The Phoenix Centre and the public toilets show what failure to attend to expressed local needs can do. Who on earth asked for a badminton court, with the disastrous acoustic consequences for what should have been intended primarily as a public hall? How could a disabled person find, let alone *use* the loos?

10 Westow Street

A new shop front, one of the first conservation conscious modernisations in the triangle

Bromley's proposals are not without controversy: the London Borough of Southwark has objected to some aspects of Bromley's plans, as has Prince Charles, anxious to see that the whole community will benefit from any future changes. Actions speak louder than words, but sometimes more confusingly: Bromley's new Park furniture is more in keeping with the character

and history of the Park, but why demolish the kiosk by the roundabout which formed such a landmark for a century and which was featured in their plans as an ideal spot for an Information Centre?

We now learn of new proposals to extend the Bakerloo line to Crystal Palace as one of the possible measures for improving London's commuter services. The consequences of such a proposal need to be widely discussed.

The splendid partnership achievement of the Crystal Palace Museum, made possible by the combined efforts of the GLC on the eve of abolition, and of local authorities, businesses and above all by the efforts of the Crystal Palace Foundation is an indication of what is possible.

One new private development must be particularly mentioned; Nesbitt Square; since it indicates both confidence in the future of the Triangle and a willingness to build in a style compatible with some of

what remains of the historical past in the area. It would perhaps be churlish to dwell on the redolence of the Late – rather than the more attractive Mid-Victorian style.

The Crystal Palace area has the good fortune to have very real international connections which have continued from the days of the Palace with its concerts and

Nesbitt Square, from Westow Street.

exhibitions. The National Sports Centre attracts athletes and audiences from all over the globe. The Angloschool students come from worldwide backgrounds, as do the visitors to the Caravan Harbour. The Crystal Palace Museum and the new hotel and leisure centre proposed for the Palace site may be expected to attract more such visitors. Do we really want them to return with memories of a down-at-heel suburb consisting mainly of estate agencies and chain take-aways with a prodigious sprouting of aerials puncturing the sky-line?

So this book is not merely a record: it is a plea. Above all what we would like to see is a growing body of people who, appreciating the special character and quality of this area, are prepared to insist that what still remains of that character is not heedlessly destroyed, but sympathetically adapted or replaced.

We also extend our invitation to all others whose localities are suffering similar depredations from arbitrary and uncaring neglect or redevelopment. Look at your own neighbourhood, at what is going on under your noses. Only by an intelligent and informed public working together in partnership

with local authorities and businesses can we achieve the beneficial changes we require to make a worthwhile environment.

This means very real changes in the attitudes and actions of our various, sometimes warring, local authorities. All who love the area must work together for this aim: to make the heights of Norwood where once the Crystal Palace glittered proudly in the sun, a happy and pleasant place in which to live, work and trade.

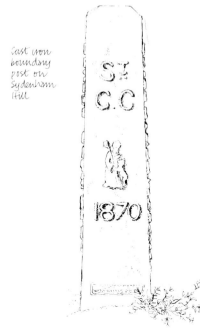

Cast iron boundary post on Sydenham Hill

S.C. C.C. 1870

'The Palace of the People'

We present these two maps as evidence of the past and the future for one of the continuing influential features of the area.

The site selected for the Sydenham Crystal Palace was a 300 acre steeply sloping site known as Penge Park and owned by one of the directors of the newly formed Crystal Palace Company. The Chairman and many of the directors were also directors of the London Brighton and South Coast Railway.

The first column of the new Palace was erected with great ceremony on 5th August 1852. It was one of the original columns from the Hyde Park building. In the socket below this column a 'time capsule' was placed containing coins newspapers and other mementoes of the occasion.

As can be seen from the plan the Crystal Palace was enormous, almost spanning the entire width of the site and with a floor area of over 600,000 square feet! The height of the main transept was 168 feet above ground level.

But for Paxton the supreme feature was to be the vast series of fountains and basins which vied with those Versailles. The size of the South Basin can be judged by the fact that the entirety of the present international standard Sports Centre stadium could be contained within it. The fountains were fed by an artesian well 575 feet deep, with water pumped uphill into a series of reservoirs and basins and finally pumped 250 feet up into the air from Brunel's prodigious towers at a rate of 7,000,000 gallons an hour.

The Palace cost an equally enormous sum of money for the times: £1,300,000.

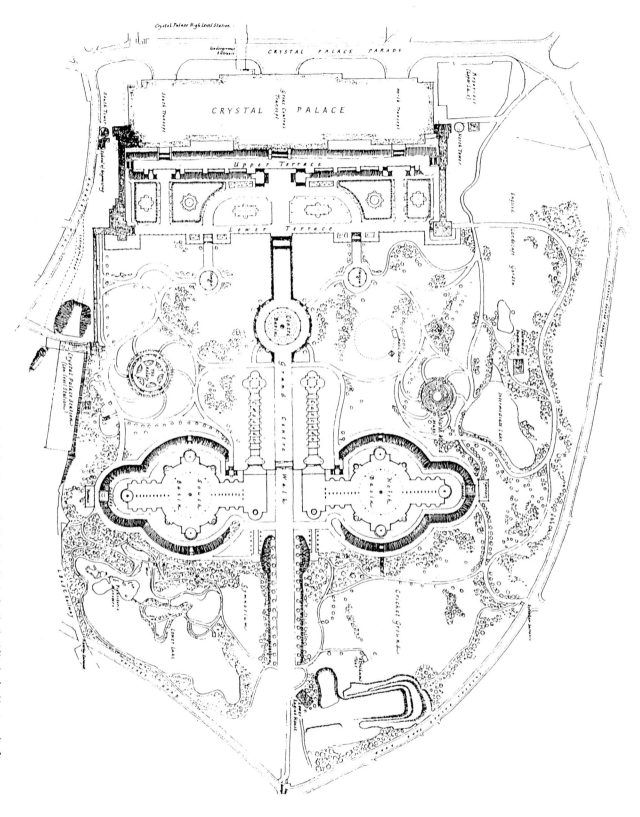

The Conversion of Penge Park: Paxton's Plan for the Crystal Palace in 1854

The Conversion of Crystal Palace Park: LB Bromley's Plan for the development of the Crystal Palace site in 1986

'The People's Park'

The London Borough of Bromley took over responsibility for the Crystal Palace Park in April 1988 following the abolition of the GLC. Bromley's Draft Development Plan published in November of that year received overwhelming support for its objectives and aims. Essentially the Plan preserved and indeed emphasised the symmetry of Paxton's scheme.

The Development Plan included proposals for improvement to all existing entrances and the creation of a new entrance to the Sports Centre. The planting and overall landscaping of the park would create a unified scheme, and involve the re-siting of the Caravan Harbour.

Many features of the original park were to be restored or re-created, including the Maze, the base of the North Tower and the Geological exhibit.

In 1988 the construction of the new Penge entrance and the improved Fisherman's Gate was started. The improvement to the perimeter walling of the grounds of the former 'Vale' was started as well.

The first phase of the Heritage and Nature Trail was to be opened in July as was the reconstructed Maze. The reconstruction of the original Rustic Bridge near the Waterfall started. The South-west corner of the site was cleared and landscaping started to provide a garden and sitting area within this part of the Park.

The restoration of the Terraces by English Heritage proceeds apace and by the time this book is published the three contenders for the development of part of the original Palace site as a Leisure Complex/Hotel/Conference Centre will have learned from Bromley which of them has been successful. All three proposals incorporate distinctive 'Crystal Palace' features.

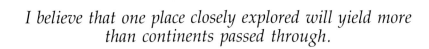

I believe that one place closely explored will yield more than continents passed through.

Lucy M. Boston from *Stranger at Green Knowe*

ABOUT THE PUBLISHERS
Would you like to join us?

Crystal Palace Triangle Community Association (CPTCA)
A Registered Charity No 261790

The area centered on the Crystal Palace triangle formed by Church Road, Westow Hill and Westow street is one of unique character in London.

Founded in 1970 with the assistance of the National Federation of Community Associations, the CPTCA has the aims of co-operating with other local interested bodies in protecting, preserving and improving the character and amenities of the area and to provide facilities for enriching the leisure time of all age-groups.

For further details, contact the **Membership Secretary, 14 Glyn Close, Grange Hill, South Norwood, SE25 6DT. Tel: 01-653 3974.**

The Croydon Society
A Registered Charity No: 270491

Aims for Protection, Preservation, Development of **your** local amenities

We hold regular meetings, talks and social events.

We arrange conducted walks and trips in the summer.

We run Working groups concerned with Planning, Transport and Natural Amenities in Croydon.

We publish our own journal, *CROYDON FOCUS*, leaflets and local history books; we sell publications.

We organise exhibitions and provide educational support.

**We Care about Croydon....
..... DO YOU?**

For further information contact the **Membership Secretary, Flat 2, 30 Howard Road, South Norwood, London SE25 5BY Tel: 01-654 6454**